REMEMBER THE 60s

This edition first published in the UK in 2006
by Green Umbrella Publishing

Printed and bound in Italy

ISBN: 1-905009-64-X
ISBN-13: 978-1-905009-64-0

REMEMBER THE 60s

Edited by Michael Heatley

Written by Alan Clayson, Chris Mason, Ian Welch and Claire Welch

1969 1968 1967 1966 1965 1964 1963 1962 1961 1961

CONTENTS

REMEMBER THE SIXTIES

1960 1961 1962 1963 1964 1965 1966 1967 1968 1969

1960

FASHION, CULTURE & ENTERTAINMENT

Ben Hur wins record 11 Oscars

This 1959 film won 11 Oscars in 1960, including: Best Actor, Charlton Heston; Best Director, William Wyler; Best Actor in a Supporting Role, Hugh Griffith; Best Art Direction-Set Decoration, Colour; Best Cinematography, Colour: Best Costume Design, Colour; Best Effects/Special Effects; Best Film Editing; Best Music, Scoring of a Dramatic or Comedy; Best Picture and Best Sound.

With a budget of $14.5 million, although the final cost was $15 million, it was at the time the most expensive movie ever made and it was set to make or

break Metro-Goldwyn-Mayer (MGM). Shooting of the epic began in Rome in May 1958 and took nine months to finish on the largest outdoor set ever built at the time.

The story centres around Judah Ben-Hur, played by Charlton Heston, who lives as a rich Jewish prince and merchant in Jerusalem at the beginning of the first century. Having been happily reunited with his old friend Messala, who arrives as commanding officer of the Roman legions, he is angry to find that their political differences pull them apart. An unfortunate incident sees Messala send Judah to the galleys and his family to prison – however, Judah vows to take revenge.

With his chiselled features, Charlton Heston was the obvious choice for the title role, and with the

Below and above: Charlton Heston the star of Ben Hur and also pictured steering his chariot in the classic race from the film.

only time he set foot in the UK was when the plane from Germany landed at Prestwick Airport, 32 miles from Glasgow. During the Second World War, Prestwick Airport developed into a major airport particularly for the delivery of American aircraft under the Lend Lease programme, up to 300 aircraft arriving daily for onward delivery.

Elvis served his country like any other GI and had no special privileges during his time in the Army. He had worried that the two years of national service would damage his musical career, but in late March 1960 he had his first post-Army recording session – some of the work was for the album 'Elvis Is Back!' Later that same month, Elvis taped a special *Welcome Home, Elvis* edition of Frank Sinatra's ABC-TV variety show. He was paid $125,000, a record sum for such an appearance.

exceptional abilities of director William Wyler this epic film was set for success. Wyler, at the time of his death in 1981, was considered by his peers as second only to John Ford. His directorial career spanned 45 years from silent pictures to the cultural revolution of the 1970s. He was nominated 12 times for an Academy Award and won three during his career. He was also the fourth recipient of the American Film Institute's Lifetime Achievement Award.

Elvis visits the UK

Having been promoted to US Army Sergeant in January 1960, rock'n'roller Elvis Presley left Germany on 1 March on his way back to New Jersey where he was officially discharged from active duty on 5 March. The

Below: Elvis wearing his US Army uniform.

His fifth (and first post-Army film), *GI Blues* began filming in late April 1960 for Paramount with co-star Juliet Prowse. The film is a light comedy melodrama with lots of singing from Elvis who spends most of the movie in uniform. The soundtrack album for the film entered the US chart in October 1960 and soon went to Number 1. It stayed at the top spot for ten weeks, but remained on the chart for 111 weeks and was the most successful album of Elvis's entire career on the *Billboard* charts. In November 1960, *GI Blues* opened across America to big box office sales and warm reviews. It was among the 15 top grossing films of that year.

Doctor Martens

In 1945, medical doctor Klaus Maertens injured his foot while skiing in the Bavarian Alps. The injury gave him the idea of developing a shoe with an air-cushioned sole to provide extra comfort for his sore foot. This simple, yet effective design was to cause a fashion avalanche.

Dr Herbert Funck developed the idea with an old college friend and, by the late 1950s, the Dr Marten shoe was selling well under the name of Dr Maertens in Germany. The shoes were named 1460s because the first pair walked off the production line in Wollaston on 1 April 1960 after Northamptonshire-based company R Griggs & Co bought the global rights to the air-cushioned sole.

Dr Martens, Docs, or DMs as they are also known have been closely linked to more musical movements than any other item of fashion. Some of the most celebrated feet in the music industry have owned a pair – Billy

Bragg, Pete Townshend, Noddy Holder, Ian Dury, Joe Strummer, Madness, Sinead O'Connor and John Peel, to name but a few. A crack SAS team wore them during the Falklands War and even Pope John Paul II owned a white pair.

Above: Elvis on the set of 'GI Blues'.
Below: A pair of DMs.

psychology experiment but was also a practical joke. Funt would set up an odd situation, and then film people's reactions to it. He guessed that the way people reacted to unusual situations would be highly entertaining and he was proved right.

The show was intended to be good humoured and never set out to humiliate or hurt anyone's feelings. If he deemed a reaction unsuitable he would not air the tape. Often, actors would be hired to play small roles in the gags and Funt himself was prone to playing a character. At the end of each gag, Funt would reveal the set up and say 'Smile you're on *Candid Camera*', letting the unsuspecting person know where the hidden camera was located.

Candid Camera

Candid Camera, titled because it caught people candidly or off guard, featured real people reacting to set-up situations. It started long before the rise of reality TV in the 1990s and continued on and off over 45 years. Although it was first screened in the late 1940s, its huge popularity started during 1960 when it was revived for a seven-year run on TV.

The programme was the brainchild of Allen Funt, a radio writer and producer. His idea was simple. It was in part a

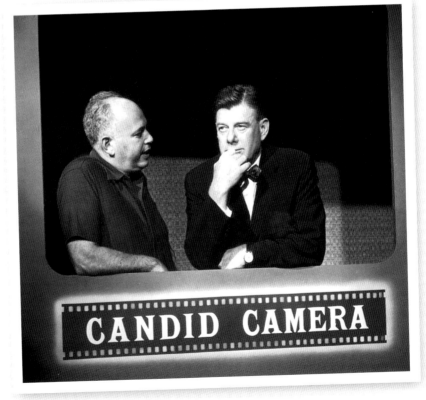

1960 1961 1962 1963 1964 1965 1966 1967 1968 1969

Below: American entertainers Allen Funt and Arthur Godfrey talk on the set of 'Candid Camera'.

1960 1961 1962 1963 1964 1965 1966 1967 1968 1969

Originally Christiansen's toys were wooden, he moved with the times and started making plastic toys when that medium started enjoying widespread use. The name was coined by Christiansen from the Danish *leg godt* which means 'play well'.

Godtfred saw the immense potential in Lego bricks as a system for creative play, but the bricks still had some technical problems as their 'locking' ability was limited. Bricks were eventually improved with hollow tubes on their underside to allow support in the base and better locking ability.

In 1960 wheels were introduced to the system which gave it the potential for building cars, trucks and other vehicles. The Lego Group as it had become, introduced toys specifically targeted towards the pre-school market and there were more than 50 sets of bricks in the Lego System of Play by this time.

Lego

Lego was first seen at the Brighton Toy Fair in 1960. The model kits were not available until the mid-1960s, but the bricks themselves immediately sold by the bucket-load. Lego was developed by a poor carpenter from Denmark, Ole Kirk Christiansen, who together with his son Godtfred turned what was a family furniture-making business for local farmers in Billund into one of the most successful toy companies in the world.

MUSIC

March

Skiffle pioneer Lonnie Donegan, a major influence on the Beatles and other British rockers with his acoustic-based music, registered his first Number 1 single in

Above: A child playing with Lego in a department store.

1957. But March 1960 saw him back on top of the UK charts for the third time with 'My Old Man's A Dustman', his modernised version of a traditional song sung by World War I troops. It was the first ever single to enter the chart at the very top, and stayed there for four weeks.

Donegan had recorded it at his record company's request the previous month at the Gaumont cinema in Doncaster but it was his typically irreverent performance on TV showcase *Sunday Night AT the London Palladium* that sent it into sales orbit. The refuse disposal union complained, but the public was clearly amused. Lonnie continued to perform the irritatingly catchy ditty until his death in 2002, explaining with a smile 'It pays the mortgage.'

Above and below: Lonnie Donegan performs with his band and poses with his guitar.

April

More popular in Europe than at home, US rock'n'rollers Gene Vincent and bosom buddy Eddie Cochran co-headlined a package tour of England's 'scream circuit' with a supporting bill that included Billy Fury, Vince Eager and other vocalists on the books of the celebrated pop svengali Larry Parnes. After the performance at the Liverpool Empire, local agent Allan Williams arranged another Merseyside spectacular with Parnes on 3 May for the two Americans – but Eddie never made it. En route by taxi from the Bristol Hippodrome to London on Sunday 17 April, a tyre burst on the A4 through Chippenham, and the speeding driver rammed a lamp post. From the back seat between his fiancée – songwriter Sharon Sheeley – and Vincent, Cochran was hurled against the roof and then out of the door.

Above: Eddie Cochran performs on the set of 'Go Johnny Go!'.
Below: Vince Eager.

Awaiting his destiny as a mid-1960s pop star, Dave Dee, who was then a police cadet, was on station duty that night, and was responsible for the deceased's possessions – including his guitar – until their removal to the USA. As the 'Man Who Killed Eddie Cochran', the chauffeur – on top of being fined and banned for dangerous driving – was, reputedly, beaten up regularly by West Country Teddy Boys.

Though a flop in the States, Cochran's forthcoming single, 'Three Steps To Heaven', was to be a posthumous UK Number 1. He was also to be the subject of a hit tribute disc, 1963's 'Just Like Eddie' by Heinz.

Moreover, despite fractured ribs and collar-bone injuries to his already calipered left leg, Gene Vincent, with characteristic obstinacy, had honoured remaining British dates in 1960, using the microphone stand as a surgical support and paying respects to his friend with a heavy-hearted 'Over

The Rainbow'. Years later he would be heard backstage addressing an unseen Cochran. When called to go on stage, he would reply sadly, 'Tell Eddie I'll be right out.'

August

Johnny Kidd and the Pirates topped the UK charts for a week with the climactic 'Shakin' All Over'. One of the few home-grown rock'n'rollers who never tried to evolve into an 'all-round entertainer', Kidd could work up a sweaty intensity known but rarely in British pop before 1962. This was enhanced by a theatrical stage act, complete with Captain Pugwash costumes, an impressive cutlass and a galleon backdrop. Moreover, he and the group's trove of hits – notably 'Please Don't Touch' and 'Shakin' All Over' – equalled anything from the annals of US classic rock.

Johnny and the Pirates were innovative too for their sparse line-up. After the wife of one of the guitarists decided she wanted him home in the evenings, Kidd did

Above: Rock'n'roll singer Johnny Kidd with his wife Jean Heath.
Below: Music impresario Larry Parnes.

not seek a replacement, preferring the simpler expedient of continuing with just bass, drums and *one* guitar. In doing so, a prototype was patented – because the Big Three, the Who, Led Zeppelin, Motörhead, the Sex Pistols and other diverse entities reliant on an instrumental 'power trio' were all traceable to the Pirates.

September

It is interesting to note how often the Grim Reaper made the charts, and the vast number of artists who released a 'death disc'. One of pop's hardiest forms, it is also perhaps the most comic – though much of the humour is unconscious, most conspicuously in the *kitsch* melodramas of the early 1960s.

In summer 1960 – probably the optimum moment in this golden aeon of death discs – 'Tell Laura I Love Her' swept into international Top Tens, either in original form by Ray Petersen or via a plenitude of indigenous covers. The lyrical thrust was that Laura's boyfriend Tommy – the first-person narrator – wants to give her 'everything', namely 'flowers, presents but most of all a wedding ring'. In hopes of affording these, he enters a stock-car race for a cash prize, but dies in a subsequent smash-up – but not before imparting giving the sentiments of the title to his beloved.

Petersen's version of the song wasn't issued in Britain after an excerpt was played on a BBC news programme to illustrate the furore in the US 'Bible Belt' by those who considered it un-Christian. However, an arrangement by Welshman David Spencer eclipsed one by John

Below: Television actor and pop singer John Leyton.

saxophone mouthpiece. Other chart-riding North Americans included Duane Eddy booming the melody of 'Because They're Young' solely on the lower strings of his 'twangy guitar'; the Piltdown Men with horn-laden 'Macdonald's Cave', follow-up to their robust overhaul of Rossini's 'William Tell Overture' (as 'Piltdown Rides Again'), and the Ventures, fighting the John Barry Seven's treatment of their 'Walk Don't Run' *magnum opus*.

The most omnipotent British instrumental group, The Shadows, were represented by 'Apache', slipping from the chart after a long reign at the top, but set to be voted Top Record of 1960 in the annual *New Musical Express* readers' poll, and destined to remain evocative of the era's provincial youth clubs with soft drinks, ping-pong and with-it vicars.

Leyton to reach Number 1 after Spencer renamed himself 'Ricky Valance' (to remind consumers of Ritchie Valens, killed the previous year in the same crash landing as Buddy Holly and the Big Bopper), and despite the BBC refusing airplay in view of a spate of recent British motor-racing fatalities. It was to be David-Ricky's only hit.

An 'answer' to record 'Tell Laura I Love Her' was to be heard before 1960 was out in a certain Marilyn Michaels' desperate 'Tell Tommy I Miss Him' – also recorded by Laura Lee and, in 1961, Skeeter Davis – which places our grieving heroine in the chapel in apparent spiritual communication with Tommy.

November

For one week, instrumentals filled an unprecedented *nine* positions in the UK Top 30. At Number 5, 'Rockin' Goose' by Ohio's Johnny and the Hurricanes featured the apposite if technically unchallenging squawk of a

15

Above: Johnny and the Hurricanes in classic 60s pose.
Below: American rock'n'roll guitarist Duane Eddy.

1960 1961 1962 1963 1964 1965 1966 1967 1968 1969

1960 1961 1962 1963 1964 1965 1966 1967 1968 1969

SPORT

Rome Olympics

While the first Olympic Games of the modern era were held after an interval of more than 1,500 years in Athens in 1896, the games held in Rome could claim to be the first truly modern spectacle due to the coverage by more than 100 television channels that brought it to a worldwide audience.

Making the most of the country's rich history, the wrestling competition was held in the Basilica of Maxentius with other ancient sites hosting gymnastics (Caracalla Baths) and the finish of the marathon (the Arch of Constantine).

Held in the Mediterranean summer heat against medical advice, the Games were not without

Above: *The women's Olympic 100m race won by Wilma Rudolph, with Dorothy Hyman taking silver.*
Below: *Cassius Clay wins Olympic gold.*

controversy. Danish cyclist Knut Jensen collapsed and died during a road race and was later found to have taken a stimulant. These were also the last games that South Africa was allowed to participate in due to Apartheid (they were re-admitted in 1992).

Notable winners in Rome included the light-heavyweight on the balance beam. Ethiopian long distance runner Abebe Bikila won the marathon barefoot to register Africa's first ever track and field gold medal while Wilma Rudolph claimed the women's sprint double (100m and 200m). What is remarkable about her feat is that as a child, the American suffered from polio and could not walk properly until the age of eight.

British success stories at these Games were few and far between: Anita Lonsborough won the women's 200m breaststroke and Don Thompson triumphed in the men's 50 kilometre walk. Dorothy Hyman took silver in the women's 100m and bronze in the 200m.

1960 1961 1962 1963 1964 1965 1966 1967 1968 1969

American boxer Cassius Marcellus Clay Jr who took gold. Clay would later turn professional, change his name to Muhammad Ali and dominate the boxing scene for much of the next two decades.

Czechoslovakia spoiled Russia's clean sweep of the women's gymnastics when Eva Bosáková claimed gold

Francis Chichester sets new Atlantic record

On 21 July, Francis Chichester sailed into New York to break the record for a solo Atlantic crossing. His 39-foot sloop, *Gipsy Moth III* (continuing the series named after his plane), had left Plymouth 40 days earlier and had

Above: Abebe Bikila runs barefoot towards victory in the Olympic marathon.

1960 1961 1962 1963 1964 1965 1966 1967 1968 1969

battled against hurricane-strength winds during the voyage that wiped 16 days off the previous best. (He would later set another record of 33 days for this crossing in 1962.)

Born in Shirwell, North Devon, on 17 September 1901, Chichester emigrated to New Zealand at the age of 18 where he co-founded a number of timber, real estate and aviation companies. He returned to England in 1929 and learnt to fly, capping this achievement with the first solo flight across the Tasman Sea two years later in a Gipsy Moth aeroplane that had been converted into a seaplane. He became the first holder of the Johnson Memorial Trophy on completing this feat.

He made the first long distance solo flight in a seaplane when he flew from Australia to Japan, although this nearly ended in tragedy when he was badly injured after hitting an overhead cable and crashing into Katsuura Harbour.

Having been diagnosed with lung cancer in 1958 and given just six months to live, Francis Chichester spent much of the 1960s pitting himself against the elements in further Atlantic crossings and an epic

Above and below: Sir Francis Chichester waves from the deck of 'Gipsy Moth' on his arrival in Sydney and receives his knighthood from the Queen.

round-the-world voyage. He was knighted in 1967 in a public ceremony where Queen Elizabeth II used the very sword that Queen Elizabeth I had given to Plymouth's other great seafaring hero, Sir Francis Drake.

Diagnosed with cancer again in 1971, illness struck after he began his fourth single-handed Transatlantic race the following year and Sir Francis Chichester KBE died in Plymouth on 26 August 1972.

He was honoured in 1979 in the Navigators Memorial plaque at Westminster Abbey. This features the vessels and routes of three great English circumnavigators: Sir Francis Drake, Captain James Cook and Sir Francis Chichester.

First Paralympic Games held

Following on from the Summer Olympics, the first ever Paralympic Games were held in Rome between 18 and 25 September 1960 emphasising the participants' athletic achievements rather than their disability. The USA topped the gold medal chart with 29 with Great Britain coming second with 19.

One of the main differences between that competition and today's is that it was open to those suffering from a spinal cord injury. The origins of the idea can be traced back to Sir Ludwig Guttmann who organised a competition for English World War II veterans with a spinal cord injury in 1948.

Athletes with other disabilities were added at the Toronto Paralympics in 1976 (the same year the first Winter Paralympics took place in Sweden) and the Games today encompass competitors from six different disability groups: amputee, cerebral palsy, intellectual disability, vision impaired, wheelchair and *les autres* (a French term used to describe other athletes with locomotive disorders).

POLITICS & CURRENT AFFAIRS

Wind of change

Although he was a Conservative of the old school, Harold Macmillan, who had become Prime Minister in 1957 following the resignation of Anthony Eden, was capable of radical thought. 'Supermac' as he was affectionately known, foresaw many of the changes which were going to affect society in the years to follow, and in particular those which would affect Britain's colonies and former colonies. In February 1960 he gave an address to the South African Parliament which was to become known as the 'Wind of Change' speech.

Below: Harold Macmillan inspecting a guard of honour of the First Kings Rifles in Lusaka, Rhodesia.

1960 1961 1962 1963 1964 1965 1966 1967 1968 1969

1960 1961 1962 1963 1964 1965 1966 1967 1968 1969

Speaking to an audience mainly consisting of supporters of the infamous Apartheid regime, he made the following observation: 'The most striking of all the impressions I have formed since I left London a month ago is the strength of African national consciousness. The wind of change is blowing through this continent, and whether we like it or not, this growth of national consciousness is a political fact.'

Needless to say, Macmillan's speech did not go down well with the South African premier, Dr Verwoerd, who made much of the rights of his white countrymen in his reply. The speech did however reverberate around the world, and in a very short time it proved to be prophetic. Little more than a month later, police opened fire on a crowd of about 5,000 Africans who were protesting against the pass laws in the township of Sharpeville. 69 protestors were killed, and a further 180 injured. Like Macmillan's speech, news of the massacre was to quickly spread around a horrified world.

South Africa left the British Commonwealth in 1961, and Verwoerd was assassinated in 1966. It took many years, but eventually Nelson Mandela was released from his prison on Robin Island and South Africa was set to begin the tortuous process of becoming a democratic state with majority rule.

Lady Chatterley on trial

In 1959 the government introduced an Obscene Publications Act. One provision of the Act was that, although a book may be thought by some to be obscene, if it had 'redeeming social merit' its publication might be allowed. DH Lawrence had written *Lady Chatterley's Lover* in 1928, and the sexually

explicit nature of the novel had ensured that an unexpurgated edition had never seen the light of day in Britain. In 1960 however, Penguin Books decided to print 200,000 copies of it and challenge the Director of Public Prosecutions to prosecute.

The Director of Public Prosecutions clearly thought the book was far too rude, and presumably considered that it had no redeeming social merit, so he took up the challenge. The result was that *Lady Chatterley* went on trial at the Old Bailey – and the whole nation wanted to get hold of a copy. The trial lasted for six days, with the defence producing a variety of witnesses ranging from bishops to an array of leading literary figures of the day. The prosecution had difficulty in making much of a case, and the clincher for the jury probably came when prosecution counsel, one

Above and below: Author of 'Lady Chatterley's Lover' DH Lawrence and two copies of the book, ruled not obscene by a jury at the Old Bailey ready for sale.

Mervyn Griffith-Jones, asked: 'Is it a book you would wish your wife or servants to read?'

Lady Chatterley was duly found innocent, and bookshops were at once besieged. Foyles, London's largest bookshop at the time, sold 300 copies in a quarter of an hour, and immediately placed an order for another 3,000. Everyone wanted to know just what Lady C had got up to with Mellors the Gamekeeper and, provided you could get hold of a copy, it would only cost you 3/6d (17.5 pence). Prosecution on the grounds of obscenity was going to be a lot more difficult in future.

World's first woman Prime Minister

Almost nine years before Golda Meir became Prime Minister of Israel, and a full 19 years before Margaret Thatcher took up residence in Downing Street, Sri Lanka (then known as Ceylon) appointed the world's first elected female Prime Minister. Mrs Sirimavo Bandaranaike, leader of the socialist Sri Lanka Freedom Party, was 44 years old. She came from a wealthy family and had taken over the leadership of the party from her husband, who had been assassinated by a Buddhist monk the previous year.

The Freedom Party, which was committed to nationalisation and educational reform, was elected with a large majority in July 1960. The energetic Mrs Bandaranaike, who was known as the 'Weeping Widow', also appointed herself as Foreign Minister and Minister of Defence. Her party was in and out of government over the years and the weeping widow died, aged 84, in the year 2000.

Below: Mrs Sirimavo Bandaranaike, widow of the assassinated Prime Minister of Ceylon campaigns for the Freedom Party.

1960 1961 1962 1963 1964 1965 1966 1967 1968 1969

1961

FASHION, CULTURE & ENTERTAINMENT

Yves St Laurent

In 1961, Yves St Laurent split from Dior, where he had been chief designer following the death of Christian Dior in the 1950s, and in January of that year showed his first collection under his own name. He also opened 160 boutiques called 'Rive Gauche' and, although not particularly renowned for being an innovative designer, he was the first couturier to develop ready-to-wear clothes on a large scale.

Born in Algeria, St Laurent is most famous for what, in his day, would have been considered outrageous gender-bending outfits and sowing the seeds for power

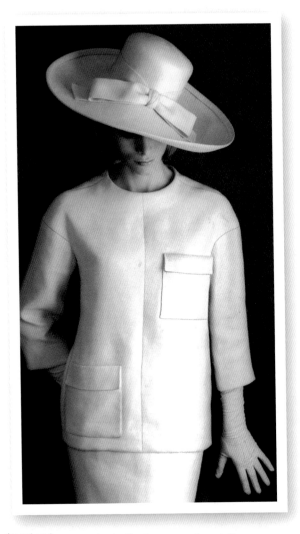

dressing for example, in the trouser suit and dinner jacket for women. He was also the first designer to effectively mix orange, pink and red, violet with yellow and black with brown. His maverick skill at capturing the mood of the moment continued after the split with Dior and the beginning of his partnership with Berge.

The first YSL tuxedo for women surfaced five years after he traded under his own name and the garment (from his autumn/winter collection) became a fashion landmark. Admirers of YSL say his style epitomised cool chic, very much in the footsteps of another legendary designer, Coco Chanel, but upon his retirement in 2002 he was criticised for not keeping up with changing trends over the past two decades.

Above: A two piece in heavy white linen designed by Yves St Laurent.
Below: Yves St Laurent examining swatches of material in his office.

He sold the YSL brand to Gucci, owned by Francois Pinault, in 1999 and there have been recriminations ever since. When the YSL brand was sold to Gucci, St Laurent and Berge kept control of the fashion house which belongs to French tycoon Pinault.

The year before his split from fashion house Dior, YSL spent six weeks in hospital after a breakdown and, over the years, he binged on drink or drugs for long periods. Despite conquering his addictions he remained a heavy smoker. Yves Saint Laurent was made a commander of the Legion of Honour by President Jacques Chirac.

Coronation Street is born

With the working title of *Florizel Street*, the concept of a soap opera from the 'grim' north was not expected to flourish. Executives were against the idea and even the man in charge of production was dubious about writing cheques for a show about the everyday lives of a group of Northerners whom he felt would hold no appeal for the audience. Meanwhile, someone in Granada Television's offices allegedly pointed out that the title sounded a bit like a toilet cleaner so the original name was dropped. Luckily for *Corrie* fans the world over, the soap, unlike its first name, did not end up down the pan.

The show made a brief appearance in 1960 to see what audience reaction would be and went nationwide under the title of *Coronation Street* for the first time in 1961. For the first month the new audience were treated to the characters establishing themselves: the woman running the corner shop retired after 30 years behind the counter; Elsie Tanner's son came home from

Below: Chris Stanford and Pat Phoenix as Dennis and Elsie Tanner, in a scene from 'Coronation Street'.

1960 1961 1962 1963 1964 1965 1966 1967 1968 1969

1960 1961 1962 1963 1964 1965 1966 1967 1968 1969

episode was shot straight afterwards. Despite earlier scepticism from the powers that be, by the end of its first year the show was the most highly rated in the country and the nation had taken the likes of Elsie, Ken and Ena Sharples to their hearts.

The soap is set in fictional Weatherfield, a part of Manchester, and portrays ordinary working class people in ordinary (most of the time) situations. *Coronation Street* is the brainchild of writer Tony Warren who was inspired by his grandmother's surroundings in inner city Salford. Today, *Coronation Street* is the longest-running soap opera in the world.

Borstal and her daughter left her Russian husband Ivan and then went back to him; Ken Barlow introduced himself by embarking on his first ill-fated romance; and another character died.

Originally the show was aired twice a week. Friday's episode was shown live and the following Monday's

One millionth Morris Minor built

The one millionth Morris Minor to roll off the assembly line appeared on 3 January 1961. It was the first British

Above: Wearing her famous hairnet, actress Violet Carson in character as Ena Sharples.
Below: A 1960s Morris Minor 1000.

car ever to reach this landmark number and to mark the auspicious event, 349 replicas of the one millionth car were built. They were finished in lilac paint, had white and gold leather seats and special 'Minor 1,000,000' badges were made for the bonnet and boot. Minor Millions have a cult following and more than forty are known to have survived.

Improvements were small and sparingly introduced. In 1961, the car's semaphore signal arms disappeared and the passenger glove box had its lid removed. The

included a larger clutch, larger drums at the front, a more efficient heater and improved rear lights.

The Avengers

The Avengers made its debut on British television in January 1961, and during its eight-year reign, aired 161 episodes. The series is a stylish blend of espionage, fantasy and quasi-science fiction.

It eventually reached audiences in 120 countries because much of the show's international popularity

following year, the Minor 1000 received an upgrade in the form of the 1098cc engine. Although it improved power output, the change to the back axle ratio meant that top speed did not increase. Other improvements

was due to co-stars Patrick Macnee as John Steed and Diana Rigg as Emma Peel.

What makes the absurd plots so endearing is the chemistry between Steed and Peel, especially because of

Above: Diana Rigg with her co-star Patrick Macnee filming an episode of 'The Avengers'.

1960 1961 1962 1963 1964 1965 1966 1967 1968 1969

the droll observations they make about their circumstances, no matter how dire. John Steed remained the leading character and ended up with six different crime-fighting partners during the series' history.

Its cult following is kept alive by those that remember the witty, off-beat television and who don't mind the dated plot-lines. It went on to become the most popular television series of all time which is a record that still stands today.

Mothercare

Established in 1961, Mothercare is now a widely recognised brand name around the world and is a market leader for new and expectant parents. The stores and mail-order operations in the UK serve customers from more than 130 countries around the world.

Mothercare sells absolutely everything that a parent will need from maternity wear, clothes for babies and children to car seats, cots, pushchairs, feeding accessories, toys and books. Its products are also affordable and it works in conjunction with Bounty to provide information to expectant mothers.

Mothercare started operating outside the UK in 1984, working with international franchise partners. The franchises recreate the concept of the UK stores, with the same store design and products and offering the same high level of customer service. In 1996, the Storehouse Group was proud to be presented with the Queen's Award for Export Achievement for its commitment to overseas franchising.

MUSIC

February

Formerly Liverpool's principal jazz haven, the Cavern was to become as famous a city landmark as the Pier Head after the Beatles – then with Pete Best on drums – made their first appearance there during one of the

new lunchtime sessions that were maximising the cellar club's profits since it had hosted its first all-pop event in May 1960. The group was re-booked on 21 March, an off-peak evening, as guests of the resident Swinging Blue Genes (later, the Swinging Blue Jeans). The Beatles subsequently performed more than two hundred

Above: The Beatles perform in the early days, (left to right) George Harrison, John Lennon, Paul McCartney, and original drummer Pete Best.

Shook The World'. That phrase would also adorn a plaque on the site of the original Cavern, demolished in 1973 to the chagrin of the English Tourist Board after pop's history became as lucrative as its present.

May

Del Shannon topped the US Hot 100 with the self-penned 'Runaway', which was conspicuous for an instrumental solo – by co-writer Max Crook on Musitrom organ – that endured as one of the most memorable in pop, and Del himself swerving cleanly into his trademark falsetto during the chorus. It reached Number 1 in Britain the following month.

Born Charles Westover in 1939, this square-jawed hunk from Michigan continued a best-selling exploration of small town soul-torture with the ilk of 'Hats Off To Larry', 'Little Town Flirt' and 'Two Silhouettes'. Other global chartbusters included 'Swiss Maid', 'Handy Man' and 1964's million-selling 'Keep Searchin''. Shannon was also remarkable for an understated image and cautious business acumen. While advised by payroll courtiers, he was no corporation marionette like so many other pop icons of the day. Indeed, throughout a career that ended with apparent suicide in 1990, he maintained an intense interest in every link of the chain from studio to pressing plant to marketplace.

times at the venue before a final show there on 3 August 1963.

Three years later, the Cavern was hosting poetry readings and similarly arty *soirées* as well as rock. It also kept a ritual weekly 'Beatle Hour' of records spun in regretful affection for the departed 'Four Lads Who

1969 1968 1967 1966 1965 1964 1963 1962 1961 1960

September

Religious piety was considered a regrettable eccentricity in 1950s rock'n'rollers like Jerry Lee Lewis and Little Richard, who were both prone to bouts of loud evangelism. Richard, however, put action over words in 1957 via a sudden renunciation of mainstream showbusiness and enrolment in a theological college. As a recording artist, he issued virtually nothing but sacred material until the mid-1960s.

Nonetheless, in 1961, he commenced what was meant to be a gospel tour of the world, but by the time it reached Europe, the set contained little but 'Tutti Frutti', 'Rip It Up' and further rock classics. Even so, the 'Georgia Peach' of old with his billowing drapes and overhanging pompadour was now a soberly attired, bristle-scalped

exquisite who was noticed crossing himself devoutly before venturing onstage.

Among his accompanists was a 15-year-old organist named Billy Preston, a black Texan who, following a British chart debut with 'That's The Way God Planned It' in 1969, was to notch up two US chart-toppers of more secular persuasion in the 1970s.

October

It was a triviality that began one of the most crucial liaisons in pop. At Dartford railway station where London dissolves into Kent, amateur guitarist and Sidcup Art College student Keith Richards boarded a commuter train and by the merest chance slid open the door of the same second-class compartment where 18-year-old

Above: Little Richard.
Below: Singer and pianist Jerry Lee Lewis.

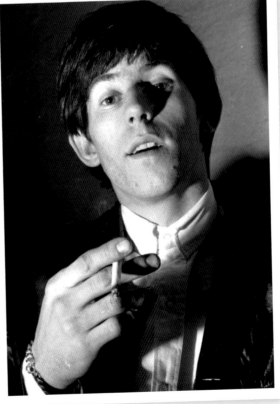

called themselves 'Little Boy Blue and the Blue Boys'. Why didn't Keith come along to the next rehearsal?

As the group had an embarrassment of guitarists, Jagger elected to concentrate on lead vocals while Richards came to play an increasingly more lively part in the activities of an outfit with no other aim than 'to turn people onto the blues,' outlined Keith, 'If we could turn them onto Muddy, Jimmy Reed, Howlin' Wolf and John Lee Hooker, then our job was done.'

From these exploratory stumblings, however, the Rolling Stones – with Mick and Keith as the creative pivots – would take shape. Into the bargain, Dick Taylor left the group in 1962 and formed the Pretty Things, who were briefly on terms with the Stones and, were to record 'SF Sorrow', unquestionably the first 'rock opera'.

Mick Jagger, on a degree course at the London School of Economics, was seated already.

They had attended the same primary school, but might have exchanged hardly a sentence during the stop-start journey had not Keith glimpsed Chuck Berry's 'Rocking At The Hop' on top of some LPs that Mick had under his arm. Richards didn't simply like Chuck Berry, he adored him – and it was with some astonishment that he asked about this vinyl treasure, which was obtainable only on import. Keith could perfectly understand why someone might give up five years of his life to own that record.

Of ensuing remarks that weren't directly to do with 'Rocking At The Hop', 'The Best Of Muddy Waters', 'Go Bo Diddley!' and Mick's other albums, it transpired that they had a mutual friend in Dick Taylor, who was mucking about with Mick and some other fellows who

Above and below: A young and fresh looking Mick Jagger and Keith Richards.

1960 1961 1962 1963 1964 1965 1966 1967 1968 1969

November

After skiffle faded in the late 1950s, many of its former participants were seen next in traditional jazz – 'trad' – bands on a growing network of clubs where watching enthusiasts were likely to know more about the music's history than did the players. The 'jazz' content in some numbers was frequently negligible because, if some black originator from New Orleans had recorded a particularly definitive solo, it was sometimes thought prudent to learn it note-for-note for regurgitation at every public performance. It was not unknown for purists to boo if a trad outfit deviated from prescribed Louisiana precedent by including saxophones or committing the more cardinal sin of amplification.

By 1961's cool, dry autumn, however, trad had spread from the intellectual fringe to a proletariat where the *Daily Express* reported teenage girls fainting to the toot-tooting of Humphrey Lyttelton, and 'ACKER' was

Below: Chris Barber (with trumpet) and his jazz band performing with Lonnie Donegan.

studded on the backs of leather jackets where 'ELVIS' had once been. So many venues became biased towards trad that it was small wonder that disenfranchised groups from every region in the kingdom responded to demands from Hamburg, Marbella and elsewhere *sur le continent* for cheap rock'n'roll labour.

Acker Bilk, Chris Barber, Kenny Ball and other jazzers each breached the Top 20 – with Somerset clarinetist Bilk's 'Stranger On The Shore' coming within an ace of Number 1. As Acker's Paramount Jazz Band went in for striped brocade and bowler hats, so matching Donegal tweeds, Confederate Army regimentals and even Roman togas and laurel wreaths would be among the uniforms of lesser units with bland banjo players, a confusion of front-line horns and 'dads' who thought that a hoarse monotone was all you needed to sing like Louis Armstrong.

The likes of the Massed Alberts and the chart-topping Temperance Seven – produced by George Martin – were only marginally jazz, but still appeared on television programmes like the BBC's opportunist *Trad Tavern* – as the bands of Bilk and Barber did in *It's Trad Dad*, the 1962 movie that marked this extraordinary craze's climax.

Above: Acker Bilk and his Jazz Band perform on stage in front of an excited crowd.

SPORT

Spurs win Double

Manager Bill Nicholson had assembled an exciting side that peaked during the 1960-61 season by securing the League and Cup Double. They had finished the previous campaign in third position, behind Wolves and Champions Burnley, failing to clinch the League title by just two points.

Nicholson's signings since his promotion from club coach in 1958 had included goalkeeper Bill Brown from Dundee and centre-back Dave Mackay from Hearts. These new faces, coupled with stalwarts like Danny Blanchflower, proved the linchpin of their success.

During their pre-season warm-up, Blanchflower had predicted to his chairman that the club would win the Double – but few would have put much faith in this statement. Their League campaign kicked off with 11 straight wins before a draw with Manchester City. Four more straight victories followed until Spurs lost their first game of the season, a 2-1 defeat away to Sheffield Wednesday.

The goalscoring exploits continued and by Christmas Eve, each of Spurs' first-choice forwards – Cliff Jones, John White, Bobby Smith, Les Allen and Terry Dyson – had registered double-figure tallies. The team would end the season having scored an amazing 115 League goals. By the end of the League campaign, Spurs had won 31 and drawn four of their 42 games to clinch the Division One title eight points ahead of Sheffield Wednesday.

The FA Cup trail started in January with a 3-2 home victory over Charlton Athletic in the Third Round. Crewe Alexandra and Aston Villa were despatched in the next two ties before Spurs needed a replay to overcome Second Division Sunderland. A 3-0 victory over Burnley

in the Villa Park semi-final set up a Wembley date with Leicester City.

The Foxes featured a young Gordon Banks in goal but he was unable to prevent Bobby Smith and Terry Dyson grabbing the goals that saw Spurs become the first club to win the Double since Preston in 1888-89.

Above: The 'Double' winning Tottenham Hotspur team.

World Figure Skating Championships cancelled following death of entire US team in plane crash

The first World Figure Skating Championship was held in St Petersburg, Russia, in 1896 and has been contested

every year since apart from 1961 (although no Championships were held during the First and Second World Wars).

The entire United States team was on board the Belgian Sabena Flight 548 from New York to Brussels en route to the 1961 World

Championships in Prague, Czechoslovakia. The pilot was forced to circle Brussels airport while waiting for a smaller plane to clear the runway, but when the Boeing 707 began to make its landing approach it crashed into a nearby field. The FAA has never determined the definitive cause of the crash that killed all 72 people on board and one person on the ground.

All 18 US athletes – including nine-times US ladies Champion Maribel Vinson-Owen – family members, coaches and officials perished in the tragedy and the Championships were immediately cancelled.

Angela Mortimer v Christine Truman in all-British Wimbledon Final

Britain was guaranteed a women's Wimbledon Champion for the first time since 1937 when Angela

Below: The Spurs skipper Danny Blanchflower holding aloft the FA Cup.

1960 1961 1962 1963 1964 1965 1966 1967 1968 1969

1960 1961 1962 1963 1964 1965 1966 1967 1968 1969

Mortimer and Christine Truman met in the first all-English Final for 47 years.

Sixth-seed Truman was the favourite but the youngster suffered an injury after she fell during the match. Having won the first set 6-4, she limped through the second, losing 4-6 and could not overcome seventh-seed Mortimer in the deciding 5-7 set.

Florence Angela Margaret Mortimer, born on 21 April 1932 in Plymouth, hadn't started playing tennis until the age of 15. She was partially deaf but she had a tremendous forehand shot.

It was her second Centre Court Final, having lost to Althea Gibson in 1958, but she had claimed Grand Slam titles in the 1955 French Championship, the 1958 Australian Championship and won the Wimbledon Doubles crown in 1955. She was a Wimbledon quarter-finalist on five other occasions: 1953-54, 1956 and 1959-60.

A Wightman Cup regular – she captained the team from 1964 to 1970 and played an instrumental part in the 1960 and 1968 victories – Mortimer underwent a stapedectomy operation to improve her hearing in 1961 but never managed to recapture her halcyon days. She married former Davis Cup captain John Edward Barrett.

Christine Truman was born on 16 January 1941 and was crowned the Wimbledon Junior Champion aged 15. Having become the youngest woman to win the French Singles Championships in 1959 (a record later beaten by Steffi Graf in 1987 and then Monica Seles in 1990), Truman won the 1960 Australian Doubles title with Maria Bueno.

Although Truman won US, Italian and Swiss titles, she never bettered runner-up at Wimbledon despite reaching three semi-finals. She competed in the Wightman Cup from 1957-71, winning the trophy three times in 1958, 1960 and 1968.

Above: *Angela Mortimer with Christine Truman (left), after winning the women's singles final at the Wimbledon.*

POLITICS & CURRENT AFFAIRS

Bay of Pigs

John F Kennedy was elected the USA's youngest ever President in November 1960, and it was not long before he faced his first international crisis. In common with his predecessor, war hero General Dwight D Eisenhower, Kennedy had an abiding fear and loathing of communism. The presence of a Soviet-supported regime in nearby Cuba seemed to Kennedy and his closest supporters to pose a real threat to America, and to the rest of the 'free world'.

The USA, which had previously exerted a tremendous amount of influence in Cuba, had taken in many refugees from Fidel Castro's regime, and a large number of these Cuban exiles were anxious to free their island from the communist dictator. It seemed to the US government (and in particular to the CIA) that an invasion, ostensibly by the exiles, but in reality heavily supported by the Americans, was the best way to get rid of Castro.

The Bahia de Cochinos (Bay of Pigs) in south-west Cuba was selected for the invasion's starting point – but it all went horribly wrong. When the beaches were stormed, the Cuban forces proved to be far more resilient than

expected, and there were many casualties on both sides. At least 114 exiles were killed, and hundreds were captured. Some of those captured were later executed as traitors, and many more were given long prison sentences. Kennedy refused to send in the Marines to rescue the exiles for fear that such action would lead to full-scale war.

The USA had expected a general uprising on the island in support of the invasion, but that didn't happen. The result of the fiasco was simply that Cuba was pushed closer to the Soviet Union, and this in turn resulted in a later crisis which would bring the world to the brink of nuclear war.

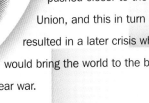

Above: Castro's troops at Playa de Citron after successfully repelling the US-backed invasion of the Bay of Pigs.
Below: John Fitzgerald Kennedy.

1960 1961 1962 1963 1964 1965 1966 1967 1968 1969

1960 1961 1962 1963 1964 1965 1966 1967 1968 1969

Berlin wall goes up

In August 1961 the world learned of the building of a wall which cut the city of Berlin in two. The city, which was geographically situated within the Soviet-dominated German Democratic Republic (East Germany), had been divided between the Eastern and Western powers since the Second World War. West Berlin remained under Allied control, and formed an isolated enclave of the country which was by now known as West Germany.

The problem for the East German government was that the citizens of East Berlin were migrating in large numbers to the West, in search of a higher standard of living and freedom from communist control. At the time,

it was estimated that about 2,000 'refugees' were leaving every day, many of them to join relations in West Berlin. Large numbers of other East Berliners were crossing the border daily, to work for the higher wages which were on offer in the other half of the city. As far as the East German government was concerned, they had to be stopped.

The wall, a concrete structure some 166 kilometres long and four metres high, was erected in record time. After it went up, there were just seven crossing points into West Berlin, where previously there had been 80. The government of the GDR euphemistically called its structure 'the anti-fascist protection wall', but naturally

Below: Soldiers building the Berlin Wall as instructed by the East German authorities, in order to strengthen the existing barriers dividing East and West Berlin.

the Berliners hated it. Even so, with Allied troops remaining in West Berlin, foreign governments did little other than to make statements to the effect that construction of the wall was an illegal and brutal act.

Before the wall was breached with the fall of communism in 1989, more than a hundred people were killed trying get over it in a bid for freedom. The fall of the Berlin Wall marked a sea change in the tide of European history.

Yuri Gagarin – first man in space

America had lost the first round of the Space Race in 1957, when the Soviet Union launched Sputnik – the world's first orbiting satellite – and they were to lose out again in 1961, when a Soviet 'cosmonaut' became the first man in space. On 12 April news came through that Yuri Gagarin, a 27-year-old Russian test pilot, had successfully orbited the Earth and landed safely on Soviet soil.

Gagarin's Vostok 1 had reached a height of 327,000 metres and his flight had lasted for 108 minutes. He had actually been forced to bail out shortly before his space vehicle landed back on earth, because it was going too fast, but the Russians didn't bother to mention that. Yuri became a Hero of the Soviet Union, and indeed a world hero. On his return to Earth, he was quoted as saying: 'Circling the Earth, I marvelled at the beauty of our planet. People of the world: let us safeguard and enhance this beauty – not destroy it.'

1960 1961 1962 1963 1964 1965 1966 1967 1968 1969

Above: Yuri Gagarin, taken during his visit to Admiralty House where he met Harold Macmillan.
Below: Soviet cosmonaut Yuri Gagarin wearing his helmet for the first ever manned flight in space.

1962

FASHION, CULTURE & ENTERTAINMENT

Dr No – James Bond

Originally based on the *James Bond* books by Ian Fleming, the films began in 1962 starring Sean Connery as agent 007. *Dr No* also starred Ursula Andress and was directed by Terence Young and had a budget of $900,000. It opened in the UK on 5 October 1962. Ever since, each film in the series begins with what is known as the James Bond gun barrel sequence which introduces agent 007.

Except in the case of *Dr No*, each film opens with a pre-credits tease, also known as the opening gambit.

Another trademark of the series is scantily clad females who can be seen doing a variety of activities in the opening credits including dancing, jumping and shooting weapons. Maurice Binder was the best known of the Bond title designers and he worked on the films from 1962 to 1989. The Bond films are also unusual in that they retain full opening and closing credits (since the 1980s it has been usual for blockbuster films to save detailed credits for the end).

The agent's introduction: 'The name's Bond, James Bond', became a catchphrase after it was first muttered by Sean Connery in *Dr No* while keeping a cigarette in the corner of his mouth. It was honoured as the twenty-second greatest cinema quotation in history by the American Film Institute in June 2005. The legendary drink of James Bond, a Martini – shaken, not stirred was actually first mentioned by Dr No himself and was only later introduced by Bond in *Goldfinger*. *Dr No* and

Above: *Sean Connery being held at gunpoint in 'Dr. No'.*

spider – the bite gave him incredible strength, a sixth 'spider' sense and the ability to climb walls and ceilings. However, he didn't use these powers to fight evil until he saw his uncle killed in a robbery.

Created by writer Stan Lee and artist Steve Ditko, Spider-Man was intended to be the 'super-hero who could be you'. The comic was a huge success and was followed by the first Spider-Man comic book, *The Amazing Spider-Man*, in March 1963.

Since he first appeared as a professional wrestler, Spider-Man has taken his crime-fighting responsibilities very seriously, the most recent resulting in three motion pictures, *Spider-Man 3* opening in May 2007. After

Thunderball (1965) are the only two films that do not have the line: 'James Bond will be back.'

In 2005, EON Productions announced that Daniel Craig had been selected as the sixth official James Bond debuted in *Casino Royale* (2006).

Spider-Man comic

The first Spider-Man comic strip was published in a magazine by Marvel Comics, *Amazing Fantasy*, issue 15 (an anthology series) in August 1962. *Amazing Fantasy* wasn't selling well and was about to be cancelled. Because no-one cared what went into the magazine, 'Spidey' was given his first outing as an experiment.

Spider-Man is an ordinary man called Peter Parker, who was bitten by a radioactive

Above: Poster for the film 'Dr. No.'
Below: The first issue of The Amazing Spider-Man comic book.

1960 1961 1962 1963 1964 1965 1966 1967 1968 1969

Anthony Burgess's novel – *A Clockwork Orange* – was immortalised on film in 1971, the style was copied and used as the basis for the thugs in the movie.

Although Teddy Boys originated in the deprived areas of London in the early 1950s, and their days were numbered in the early 1960s, young mods were taking an interest in terms of the Teddy Boys' unique fashion. It wasn't just about the clothes though – there was an entire look and hair was cut into outlandish 'duck's ass' ('DA') styles. Long jackets were juxtaposed with thin bootlace ties, while stovepipe trousers were cut short to reveal loud patterned socks. Shoes had to consist of winkle-pickers or suede brothel creepers.

Pill box hat

Jackie Kennedy, First Lady of the USA, is said to have popularised the pill box hat (so called because it looks as if it's designed to hold pills) in 1962 when she wore

months of speculation, the villain of *Spidey 3* movie was confirmed as Flint Marko, also known as Sandman. The movie will star Thomas Haden Church, Tobey Maguire, Kirsten Dunst, Topher Grace, James Franco and will be directed by Sam Raimi.

Teddy Boy suit

Teddy Boys were the original teen rebels dressed in a blend of romantic Edwardian clothes (hence the name Teddy), which included a mixture of slim coats, velvet trims and American rock'n'roll styles.

Despite the dapper image, Teddy Boys were not to be trifled with. Most carried flick knives and switchblades and some even carried cycle chains and razors. The look became synonymous with violence and Teddy Boys were thought of as cold-hearted. When

Above: A young man in a typical Teddy Boy outfit.
Below: Jacqueline Kennedy dressed in her trademark pill box hat.

one on television. However, she was not the first to wear the style – it had been a fashion accessory in different forms since the 1930s.

The hat went on to become the favoured headwear of African President Mobutu when he became head of state in 1965. With its famous admirers (actress Edie Sedgwick also wore one) and political connotations, the hat's popularity became so large that Bob Dylan released a song entitled 'Leopard-skin Pill Box Hat' in 1966.

The Pill Box is actually a small woman's hat with a flat crown and straight upright sides. The most famous pill box ever worn must be the pink hat worn by Jackie Kennedy the day her husband, John F Kennedy, thirty-fifth President of the USA, was assassinated in Dallas, Texas on 22 November 1963. Although interest in the hat was already starting to wane by this time, the sight of the First Lady cradling her husband's head in her lap after the assassination seemed to bring its popularity to an end.

Z Cars

Writer Troy Kennedy Martin was confined to bed with mumps and decided to pass the time listening to the police wavelength on his radio. The result was *Z Cars* which was first aired in January 1962. The popular series was named after the Ford Zephyr, as it was the model used as the patrol vehicles on the show.

Set on Merseyside at a time when Liverpool was on the verge of significant social change, police were being transferred off the beat and using response vehicles for the first time. It established the careers of actors such

Above: The actors of the television programme 'Z Cars'.

as: Stratford Johns, Frank Windsor, Brian Blessed, James Ellis and Colin Welland.

The show attempted to emulate the appeal of American shows such as *Highway Patrol* and had much more 'gritty' realism than previous UK police shows such as *Dixon Of Dock Green*. Close attention to police procedures, observation of behaviour and regional accents all helped the show to achieve its objective and popularity. The show eventually retired its Ford Zephyrs in September 1978, but in retrospect was the inspiration for modern cop shows such as *The Sweeney* and *The Bill*.

MUSIC

March

Guitarist Alexis Korner and another former trad jazz sideman, mouth-organist Cyril Davies founded a London venue where their Blues Incorporated, Britain's first true all-blues outfit, became resident.

Opening on St Patrick's Day in a basement between a jeweller's and a teashop along Ealing Broadway, the G Club was patronised straightaway by blues devotees and curiosity-seekers from other metropolitan suburbs. Certain listeners were players themselves, and were encouraged to 'sit in' with the loose collective over which Davies and Korner presided.

Some among the throng searched amongst themselves for kindred spirits with whom to form what would soon look and sound dangerously like beat groups, albeit without much compromising their blues (or rhythm-and-blues) determination. Among

these were subsequent Rolling Stones, Kinks, Downliners Sect-arians, Artwoods, Yardbirds and Pretty Things – as well as future members of Cream, The Nice, Pentangle, the Faces, Manfred Mann and Led Zeppelin.

April

Peter, Paul and Mary, a merger of three solo artists, was the first commercially successful 'New Left' act to emerge from Greenwich Village, New York's vibrant beatnik district where, in the early 1960s, the civil rights movement had fused with topical folk song to be labelled 'protest.' Though their lightweight style was similar to that of Britain's Springfields, the trio helped popularise the songs of performers who might otherwise have remained known only to a cult following. Among these was Bob Dylan, who was also managed by Albert Grossman. Dylan first intruded on the pop charts –

Below: Peter, Paul and Mary perform on stage.

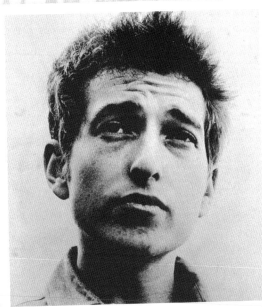

hewn intonation, untutored phrasing and eccentric breath control. Nevertheless, some had to admit that Dylan had an idiosyncratic harmonica technique and was a fair acoustic guitarist. There were few complaints too about the intrinsic content of his songs. Collectively, these embraced semi-traditional material as well as impromptu 'talking blues' and more earnest Dylan

albeit by proxy – when the trio recorded his anti-war opus, 'Blowin' in the Wind', which almost topped the US charts, and climbed to Number 13 in Britain.

By association, 21-year-old Bob's version harried the lower reaches of the US Hot 100. Three years earlier, he had been working the folk clubs in the bohemian quarter of Minneapolis, where he was attending university under his born name, Robert Allen Zimmerman. On adopting his familiar stage alias (styled after Welsh writer Dylan Thomas), he abandoned his studies to move to Greenwich Village where, via Grossman, he attracted the interest of CBS record producer John Hammond, who had also 'discovered' Billie Holliday and Bessie Smith.

Dylan's plaintive debut LP was acclaimed in the *New Musical Express* as 'most exciting', though other critics expressed little enthusiasm for his rough-

originals such as 'Blowin' In The Wind', 'Masters Of War', 'A Pawn In Their Game' and like comments on topical and socio-political issues that were outlined less skilfully by Phil Ochs, Tom Paxton and fellow mainstream folkies.

June

After years as a backroom songwriter, Carole King released a one-shot 45, 'It Might As Well Rain Until September', having been persuaded that no-one could improve upon her demo of the number. While it reached Number 22 in the USA, it penetrated Britain's Top Ten. That same month, million-selling 'The Locomotion', another King opus – co-written with then-husband Gerry

Above and below: Bob Dylan in thoughtful pose and in the studio playing the piano.

1960 1961 **1962** 1963 1964 1965 1966 1967 1968 1969

July

To mixed reviews, singing pianist Ray Charles unleashed 'Modern Sounds In Country And Western', an album of a style of music that seemed iconoclastic in view of previous offerings by one regarded by white intelligentsia as the Twisted Voice of the Underdog.

Goffin – was issued by the couple's baby-sitter, Eva Boyd (as 'Little Eva').

The demarcation line between jobbing tunesmith and recording artist was to persist well into the 1960s, even after the Beach Boys, the Beatles and other self-created rock groups with internal sources of new material gave the music industry establishment a nasty turn. In New York's Brill Building – opposite the statue of Tin Pan Alley behemoth George M Cohen in Times Square – there was even a songwriting 'factory' where King, Paul Anka, Neil Sedaka and other stars-in-embryo learnt their crafts, churning out assembly-line pop for the masses.

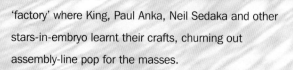

Black, blind and mainlining on heroin, Charles had been synonymous with the pop end of blues and jazz. He'd also worked with Count Basie and the Modern Jazz Quartet. As such, he was so worshipped that a British female fan offered him her eyes – and a Charles concert at London's Hammersmith Odeon in 1961 was 'one of the greatest things I've ever seen' to 16-year-old Gary Brooker, later mainstay of both the Paramounts and Procol Harum.

Other vocalists who owed much to Ray included Eric Burdon, Cliff Bennett, Van Morrison, Steve Winwood and Joe Cocker, each of them impressed mostly by a strangled vehemence of such sensitivity – 'soul' if you like – that a fractional widening of vibrato during a sustained note could be as loaded as his most anguished wail.

Above: Paul Anka.
Above right: Ray Charles.
Below: Neil Sedaka.

October

The Beatles were to leave the runway with their maiden single, 'Love Me Do'. Its recording in summer was the group's first session with Ringo Starr, who had replaced Pete Best after producer George Martin decided to hire Andy White from the Vic Lewis Orchestra to ghost the drumming.

During the allocated three hours at EMI's Abbey Road studio, Martin also imposed drastic alterations to 'Love Me Do'; made the Beatles tape a 'professional' song, 'How Do You Do It', that he'd picked to be the follow-up and, lastly, required them to return the following week because he wasn't pleased with the evening's work.

At some point during this next attempt, Martin waved in a dejected Ringo to bash a tambourine on the 'PS I Love You' flip-side. Furthermore, on several takes of 'Love Me Do', it was to be Starr rather than White behind the kit as the team neared a satisfactory result.

The tip of John Lennon and Paul McCartney's songwriting iceberg, 'Love Me Do' was to hover on the edge of the Top 20 until just after Christmas thanks to scattered airings on the radio and the buzz from the north-west.

The Beatles had done well for first timers, but few assumed then that they were more than a classic local group who could easily be back on the Merseyside-Hamburg treadmill of engagements within a year. Nevertheless, they were permitted to record John and Paul's 'Please Please Me' as the next A-side instead of the earmarked 'How Do You Do It' – which, by Gerry and the Pacemakers, was to be the first disc by a Liverpool outfit to achieve a Number 1.

At Number 2, 'Please Please Me' had been beaten by Frank Ifield's 'The Wayward Wind'. However, a third effort, 'From Me To You' eased 'How Do You Do It' from the top, and the rest, as they say, is history.

Above: The Beatles in buoyant mood.

SPORT

Chile World Cup

Brazil successfully defended the trophy they had won in Sweden four years earlier but they had to do it without the talents of star player Pelé, injured in the 0-0 group draw against Czechoslovakia.

British hopes rested with England, the only home nation to have qualified for the tournament, and they scraped through their qualifying group by beating Argentina 3-1, drawing 0-0 with Bulgaria and losing 2-1 to Hungary (Ron Flowers 2, Bobby Charlton and Jimmy Greaves were the goalscorers).

They were unfortunate to meet a Brazil side in the quarter-final who in Amarildo – dubbed 'the white Pelé' for his performances after scoring twice in his first game, against Spain – had a superb replacement for their injured superstar. A brace from Garrincha coupled with a goal from Vava proved too much for Walter Winterbottom's side and they fell 3-1 to the eventual winners.

Hosts Chile boosted national pride having come through the Battle of Santiago, a vicious clash with Italy which saw two Italians sent off although many watching believed further players should have been dismissed from both sides. Chile beat the Soviet Union 2-1 in the quarter-final before being dismissed 4-2 by Brazil in the semis with Garrincha and Vava again being the names on the scoresheet, this time with two apiece.

The other Finalists were Czechoslovakia who had seen off Hungary (1-0) and Yugoslavia (3-1) in the knockout stages. It looked as though there could be an

Above: *The Brazilian football team pose before winning the World Cup.*

1938) to win all four Grand Slam titles in the same year (he later repeated this achievement in 1969).

In the era before the Open tournaments, Laver – born on 9 August 1938 – had won the Australian Championship in 1960 and Wimbledon the following year but it was to be 1962 that shattered the records.

He met Australian Roy Emerson in three out of the four Grand Slam Finals, winning 8-6, 0-6, 6-4, 6-4 in Australia, 3-6, 2-6, 6-3, 9-7, 6-2 in France and 6-2, 6-4, 5-7, 6-4 in the US. Another Aussie Marty Mulligan was his Wimbledon opponent and Laver sailed past him in three straight sets.

He also won the Italian and German Championships that year, equalling another once-before achieved feat – the difficult clay-court triple of Paris, Rome and Hamburg – by Lew Hoad in 1956.

Graham Hill F1 Champion

Graham Hill, born in London on 15 February 1929, only learned to drive at the age of 24 but amazingly would be Formula 1 World Champion within ten years. His trademark moustache stemmed from rebelling against his National Service stint in the Royal Navy.

upset on the cards when Josef Masopust put the Czechs ahead after 15 minutes but the Brazilians responded as only true World Champions can.

Amarildo equalised just two minutes later and goals from Zito and Vava midway through the second half ensured their enjoyment of the Jules Rimet trophy would last for at least another four years.

Rod Laver wins tennis Grand Slam

Australian left-hander Rod Laver became only the second male player after Don Budge (in

Above: Rod Laver proudly holding the Men's Singles Trophy at Wimbledon.
Below: Graham Hill in his BRM car, at the Dutch Grand Prix at Zandvoort.

1950 1961 1962 1963 1964 1965 1966 1967 1968 1969

Having become obsessed with motor racing after a few trial laps around Brands Hatch in a Formula 3 car, Hill quit his job at an instrument company and joined the Brands Hatch Racing Company as a mechanic before graduating to become an instructor. On race days, he met Colin Chapman who was in the process of setting up his soon to be famous Lotus team, and by the time it entered Formula One in 1958 Hill was firmly ensconced in the outfit.

The Lotus was not fast enough for Hill and in 1960 he switched his allegiance to BRM. It was the introduction of a new V8 engine that provided BRM and Hill with the opportunity to win races in 1962 and victories in the Dutch, German, Italian and South African Grands Prix gave him the title over Lotus's Jim Clark.

Although the BRM remained competitive, Hill (winner of the 1966 Indy 500) returned to Lotus in 1967 to partner Jim Clark. Following his team-mate's death at Hockenheim, Hill led Lotus to its third and his second world title in 1968.

Although more Grands Prix wins followed – most notably a record fifth victory at Monaco – Hill failed to register a hat-trick of titles and retired in 1975 following the humiliation of failing to qualify for that year's Monaco Grand Prix. He became the only man to win motorsport's triple crown when he captured the 1972 Le Mans title to go with his victories at Indianapolis and Monaco.

He formed his own team in 1973 but was killed when the light aircraft he was piloting crashed in bad weather on 29 November 1975.

Above: Graham Hill in racing action at Silverstone.

POLITICS & CURRENT AFFAIRS

Commonwealth Immigration Act

After the Second World War, Britain was in desperate need of labour. A decision was therefore made to bring Commonwealth citizens to these shores to help with the crisis. Ironically, the Conservative MP Enoch Powell, who was later to be vilified as a racist for his 'Rivers of Blood' speech (Birmingham, 1968) was at the time in favour of the move. The first batch of immigrants to seek a new life in the mother country arrived, full of hope and expectation, at Tilbury Dock on the good ship *Empire Windrush* in 1948.

While some welcomed the new arrivals, resentment followed – especially when people began to believe that the incomers were taking their jobs and making a severe housing shortage even more acute. Over the next few years immigrants from other Caribbean countries, and from India, Pakistan and Africa followed. They made a vital contribution to the economy of war-torn Britain, but their contribution was not always recognised and resentment, especially in inner city areas, began to intensify.

In 1962 the Conservative Government decided to introduce a Commonwealth Immigration Act, which would make it harder, though by no means impossible, for people to migrate to this

1960 1961 **1962** 1963 1964 1965 1966 1967 1968 1969

Above and below: One of the last West Indian immigrants is interviewed before the Commonwealth Immigrants Act comes into place and The 'Empire Windrush' that had brought in the first batch of immigrants from the Caribbean.

country. A voucher system was introduced, with Category A vouchers issued to those who already had a job to come to, Category B vouchers available to those who, while they had no job, nonetheless had skills which were still needed, and Category C vouchers for anyone who did not fall into Categories A or B. The Category C vouchers were issued on a first come, first served basis – a strange, and very British, compromise. In subsequent years, both Conservative and Labour governments were to introduce further legislation in an attempt to restrict Commonwealth immigration.

Cuban missile crisis

About a year after the Bay of Pigs fiasco, US President John F Kennedy faced another crisis over Cuba. The Soviet Union may have been winning the space race, but it was lagging behind when it came to nuclear arms capability. The USA could aim its nuclear weapons at Russia with impunity, but the Soviets did not have the capability to strike back.

With the agreement of Fidel Castro, Soviet premier Nikita Khrushchev decided to place missiles in Cuba to deter the United States from attacking the Soviet Union, and also to prevent another invasion of Cuba. During the summer of 1962, aerial photographs showed evidence of nuclear missile sites under construction in Cuba, so JFK called together his senior advisors – including his brother, attorney general Bobby Kennedy – to plan his response. The island was to be blockaded to prevent the landing of more weapons, and dire warnings were to be issued.

On 27 October, Kennedy announced to a shocked western world that Russian missiles were in place on Cuba, and said that if any were launched from the island, then this would be regarded as an attack on the US and America would respond accordingly. While Kennedy demanded that the Soviets removed all weapons from Cuba, the world prepared itself for the distinct possibility of nuclear war. In the event, common sense prevailed. Khrushchev wrote to Kennedy, saying

LAUNC

Below: A spy photo of a missile base in Cuba, with labels detailing various parts of the camp.

that he would be prepared to withdraw if the USA guaranteed not to invade Cuba. He also wanted Kennedy to remove his missiles from Turkey. A compromise solution was eventually agreed, and the world breathed again.

The West had won, and many felt that Khrushchev had been humiliated, but the ideological differences between capitalism and communism had very nearly brought an end to civilisation as we know it.

SITION

MISSILE-READY TENTS

MISSILE ERECTORS

Eichmann hanged

SS-Obersturmbannfuehrer Karl Adolf Eichmann (born 1906) was head of the Nazi government's Department For Jewish Affairs from 1941 until 1945. Arrested at the end of the war, he was detained in an American internment camp from which, quite remarkably, he managed to escape unrecognised. He later fled to Argentina, where he lived under the name of Ricardo Klement.

Israeli Mossad agents spent many years tracking Eichmann down, and finally got their man in 1960. He was taken for trial in Jerusalem, accused of being responsible for the deportation to extermination camps of three million Jews. He barely denied the charge, saying basically that he was only following orders. Found guilty in August 1961, Adolph Eichmann was hanged in Jerusalem on 31 May 1962. His final words are reputed to have been: 'I had to obey the rules of war and my flag. I am ready.'

Above: Austrian government official Adolf Eichmann in his special bulletproof glass cage in a courtroom in Jerusalem, Israel.

1960 1961 **1962** 1963 1964 1965 1966 1967 1968 1969

1963

FASHION, CULTURE & ENTERTAINMENT

Olivia Newton-John's TV debut

Cambridge born Olivia moved to Melbourne, Australia when she was five and by the age of 15 had formed the all-girl group, Sol Four, going on to win a talent contest on the television show, *Sing, Sing, Sing* hosted by Johnny O'Keefe. In 1963, Olivia was becoming a regular face on Australian television and pop programmes such as *The Go Show*.

In 1965, Olivia moved to London and was joined by her life-long friend, whom she met through Australian television, Pat Carroll (who later married another life-long friend, John Farrar). The duo toured Europe playing nightclubs and American service bases. In 1966, Olivia released a version of Jackie DeShannon's 'Till You Say You'll Be Mine' for Decca Records and in 1971 Bruce Welch (of the Shadows) and John Farrar co-produced her version of Bob Dylan's 'If Not For You'. Olivia released her debut US album 'Let Me Be There' two years later and was rewarded with her first Top 10 single of the same name.

She became a superstar in 1978 for her role as Sandy in *Grease*, co-starring John Travolta, which led to the most successful musical movie soundtrack of all time with hits such as 'Summer Nights' and 'Hopelessly Devoted To You'. Olivia soon amassed numerous film credits including *Xanadu*, where she danced with Gene Kelly, and has even co-starred with her daughter Chloe Lattanzi in the movie *The Wilde Girls*.

Despite being diagnosed with and overcoming breast cancer in 1992, which inspired the self-penned 'GAIA', Olivia's career has spanned more than three decades and her popularity worldwide remains high. Olivia Newton-John was awarded the OBE for her services to the musical industry and charity in 1979. Today, she still has homes in the US and Australia.

Below: A youthful Olivia Newton-John.

1960 1961 1962 **1963** 1964 1965 1966 1967 1968 1969

Doctor Who

Doctor Who initially aired for the BBC on 23 November 1963 and ran until 1989. It is the longest running science fiction television series in history and was re-launched by the BBC, after many years of pressure from fans, on 26 March 2005, starring Christopher Eccleston as the Doctor and Billie Piper as side-kick Rose Tyler.

The first Doctor was played by William Hartnell, a mysterious traveller in space and time. The Doctor's trusty TARDIS, an old police telephone box, can take him and his companions to any point in time and space where inevitably they find evil.

The first episode in the series was 'An Unearthly Child', written by Anthony Coburn and directed by Waris Hussein. The story centres on schoolgirl, Susan Foreman, played by Carole Ann Ford, who seems to have superior knowledge about science and history, but little experience of everyday life.

Perplexed, her two teachers, Ian Chesterton and Barbara Wright, played by William Russell and Jacqueline Hill, follow the schoolgirl home where they find she is the granddaughter of the enigmatic Doctor. Worried they will reveal his secret – that he is an alien – the Doctor abducts Ian and Barbara and transports them back to the dawn of human history. There are actually two versions of the first episode, the original pilot and the 'official' version.

Over the years, top episodes include 'The Twin Dilemma', 'The King's Demons' and 'Arc Of Infinity'. Throughout, the evil Daleks (mutated descendants of the Kaled people of the planet Skaro) played an important role in Doctor Who's adventures with their

Above: William Hartnell stars as The Doctor alongside Dracula and Frankenstein's monster in an episode called 'The Chase'.

1969 1968 1967 1966 1965 1964 1963 1962 1961 1960

unforgettable catchphrase 'exterminate, exterminate' as they rolled after the Doctor and companions trying to annihilate them.

The ninth Doctor (Christopher Eccleston), saved the universe when he conquered the Daleks, but was killed in the process. It was left to the tenth Doctor, David Tennant, to show more of the dark sides and secrets of the universe and fight against the evil Cybermen.

The Great Escape

Starring Steve McQueen, James Garner, Richard Attenborough and Charles Bronson and directed by John Sturges, *The Great Escape* was released in cinemas in 1963 to rave reviews and is considered one of the all-time great war movies.

Allied prisoners of war were exasperating the Nazis by the number of escapees from prison camps. They relocated them to high-security, 'escape-proof' camps to sit out the remainder of the Second World War.

The Great Escape, is based on a true story of some Allied prisoners who, undaunted by the high security

surrounding them, plan one of the most ambitious escapes of the conflict.

The first half of the film concentrates on the prisoners' attempts to outwit the Nazis while building their escape tunnel while the second half of the film is devoted to high adventure as they use planes, trains and boats to escape occupied Europe.

Above: 'Exterminate' – The Daleks.
Below: Richard Attenborough, James Coburn and Gordon Jackson in 'The Great Escape'.

fashion as evening wear which caused so much controversy.

In the 1970s attitudes changed and the trouser suit was able to rise above its lowly position and it became acceptable for women to be seen on a night out in trousers. For the first time women were allowed to wear trousers in business and formal settings.

The Pant Suit

The Trouser Suit really took off in 1963 when Cathy McGowan, star of the TV music show, *Ready Steady Go* wore one on television. Until then, trousers for women had not received a good press and during the earlier years of the decade was deemed by those in high society to be beneath them and a fashion statement for working class women.

Some restaurants even refused entry to potential customers wearing one, despite the fact that women had been wearing long trousers since the 1920s. It was the fact that designers had introduced a jacket and trousers in women's

1960 1961 1962 **1963** 1964 1965 1966 1967 1968 1969

Below: Cathy McGowan in one of her early trouser suits.

1960 1961 1962 1963 1964 1965 1966 1967 1968 1969

Mop top hair

The Beatles were mainly responsible for the mop top haircut, a description which likened the style to a shaggy dish mop. The group shocked many when they turned up with dodgy bowl cuts and much controversy resulted.

The older generation considered men with long hair to be preposterous. The fact that men's hair could grow below their ears was widely seen as unacceptable,

especially in an era where men were expected to show military precision.

Of course, for the young, the mop top was extremely popular and many schools banned pupils from sporting the style. Things even went as far as cries for the government to reinstate National Service and 'stop the rot'.

But the post-war baby boom meant that there were a high number of teenagers in the early Sixties.

Employment levels were fairly high and, for the first time, teenagers had more money and more access to fashions of the day. After the Teddy Boys who, during the 1950s had made it acceptable for men to make a statement with fashion, including their hairstyles, it was only to be expected that the hairstyle sported by the biggest band in the country was going to be popular, no matter what the older generation had to say.

MUSIC

January

Despite – or because of – being on general release during one of the bitterest winters in decades, *Summer Holiday* was *the* British pop movie of 1963. It was also the fourth celluloid vehicle for Cliff Richard, who had assumed the role of principal English 'answer' to Elvis Presley since the late 1950s.

Above: Beatles drummer Ringo Starr sporting a mop top.
Below: Cliff Richard, after crowds in Leicester Square prevented him from attending the premiere of his film 'Summer Holiday'.

Cliff's first two flicks, *Serious Charge* and – also in 1959 – *Expresso Bongo* had been quite tough but, with a weather-eye on Elvis, he went soft with 1961's *The Young Ones* and *Summer Holiday*: shopworn 'teenpic' plots about 'good kids' making wholesome and purposeful whoopee. Billy Fury and Adam Faith, Richard's chief rivals, also trod the same backwards path from taut drama to the shallow 'fun' of *I Gotta Horse* (Fury) and *What A Whopper!* (Faith).

During the watershed year of 1963, however, all three adopted different vocational strategies. Faith switched without a pause from lightweight

ballads to ersatz Merseybeat, and was accompanied on television by a visible two guitars-bass-drums combo, the Roulettes. Fury too hired a state-of-the-art backing outfit, but otherwise steeled himself for the cabaret circuit where current chart status had no meaning.

Cliff, however, neither fought back nor beat a calculated retreat, recognising that however much fans of the up-and-coming beat groups loved to hate him, many pop consumers yearned for a return to the old ways. 'Are you going to let Britain's king of talent be beaten by a flash-in-the-pan group like the Beatles?' enquired a particularly volcanic Richard disciple in a letter to the *New Musical Express*. It seemed that a lot of them weren't, with the *Summer Holiday* soundtrack lingering in the album charts from January to October, even with the issue of a Richard 'best of' collection in mid-summer.

The hits kept coming, and included a 1965 Number 1 with 'The Minute You're Gone', even as the Bachelor Boy plunged deeper into variety, evangelical Christianity and Songs For Europe; made another *Summer Holiday*-esque film (*It's A Wonderful Life*) and shovelled out a greater proportion of potboiling ballads until the danger had passed.

1960 1961 1962 **1963** 1964 1965 1966 1967 1968 1969

Above: Adam Faith.
Middle: Billy Fury

March

A light aircraft flying country-and-western stars Cowboy Copas, Patsy Cline and Hawkshaw Hawkins back to Nashville after a charity concert in Kansas City crashed into the side of a mountain, killing the pilot and his passengers. On hearing the radio reports, Roger Miller and Carl Perkins joined the party searching the area near Camden, Tennessee.

The artiste most missed by a wider world was Cline, who could 'cry on both sides of the microphone'. Naturally, her heartbreak hits had figured in US music trade journal *Billboard*'s country chart, but several picked up enough sales outside this market to 'cross over' into the pop Hot 100. Chief among these was 1961's 'Crazy', which reached the Top 20 in both the States and, belatedly, the UK via its use in a TV commercial in 1990. Nine years earlier, Nashville

producer Owen Bradley's skills with sampler, vari-speed and editing block brought together Cline and Jim Reeves – who died in similar circumstances in 1964 – on disc with a duet of 'Have You Ever Been Lonely'.

April

During the hitherto-unsigned Rolling Stones' long residency in his weekly Crawdaddy club in Richmond, it was Georgio Gomelsky's foregone conclusion – a wrong one as things turned out – that he would become the group's manager. After all, as a powerful figure on the National Jazz Federation, Gomelsky had cultivated vital connections, most recently with Brian Epstein, the Beatles' manager. This manifested itself most tangibly when Georgio engineered a trip to the Crawdaddy by those very Beatles.

As he had hoped, their chart-riding peers took a liking to the Stones. Indeed, the cordiality between the two outfits that evening concluded with the Stones receiving complimentary tickets for *Swinging '63*, an extravaganza headlined by the Beatles at London's Royal Albert Hall. In the twilight afterwards, some girls

Above right: Brian Jones.
Below: Patsy Cline.

mistook Brian Jones for George Harrison, and asked for his autograph. Noting Jones's peculiar exaltation at this incident, Keith Richards was to sneer 'Brian wanted to be a pop star the minute he saw the Beatles.'

May

If far removed stylistically from the big beat, the Springfields – Londoners Mike Hurst and siblings Tom and Dusty Springfield – were voted top British vocal group for the third time in the *New Musical Express*'s readers poll, and had peaked at Number 5 with their latest single, 'Say I Won't be There', based on a traditional Gallic *chanson*.

This typified the trio's strategy of adapting well-known folk ditties, established with their very first single, 1961's 'Dear John' on which the melody of the US Civil War song 'Marching Through Georgia' was readily discernible. Nevertheless, their most enduring hit, 'Island Of Dreams' broke the formula, being a Tom Springfield original.

Signs of commercial danger were, however, soon to be perceptible when 'Come On Home', the follow-up to 'Say I Won't Be There', struggled in the lower reaches of the Top 30. Within weeks, the Springfields disbanded, and Dusty announced that her first solo 45, 'I Only

Want To Be With You', was to be released in the autumn. A star was born…

October

'We don't feel we are ready,' John Lennon had insisted during summer negotiations for his Beatles to top the bill on ITV's *Val Parnell's Sunday Night At The London Palladium*, second only to *The Royal Command Performance* as the pinnacle of British show business.

Viewing figures were at their highest when the group agreed to star on the show at last, kicking it off with a teasing burst of 'I Saw Her Standing There' during a

Above: Pop trio The Springfields, before Dusty decided to go solo.

1960 1961 1962 **1963** 1964 1965 1966 1967 1968 1969

1960 1961 1962 1963 1964 1965 1966 1967 1968 1969

single rotation of the theatre's revolving stage. Then the seated majority of teenagers fidgeted through endless centuries of formation dancing, US crooner Brook Benton, singing comedian Des O'Connor and the audience participation 'Beat The Clock' interlude.

After John, Paul, George and Ringo reappeared for five numbers that they could hardly hear themselves play above the shrieking ecstasy, the entire cast lined up for the customary finale to wave a cheery goodbye as the platform turned slowly once more. Whenever the Beatles hoved into view, the pit orchestra's sight-reading of the 'Startime' theme tune would be swamped in screams.

The next day, the media was full of the 'overnight sensation' and its aftermath as a police cordon with helmets rolling in the gutter held back hundreds of clamorous fans to allow the Beatles' getaway car to drive off. One pressured reporter – Vincent Mulchrone of the *Daily Mirror* – chronicling the mayhem came up with 'Beatlemania'. The word stuck, but Beatlemania as a phenomenon was to have less to do with the group itself than the behaviour of the British public who, once convinced of something incredible, would believe it with an enthusiasm never displayed for mundane fact.

Fun for all the family, the Beatles were now part of the national furniture. Like Tommy Steele and Cliff Richard before them, they'd be ideal for pantomime, charity football matches and children's television. Maybe they'd develop into a sort of updated Crazy Gang when they were overtaken – as they surely would be – by another short-lived 'mania'.

Above and below: Screaming Beatles fans and the 'Fab Four' backstage after their 'Sunday Night at the London Palladium' show.

SPORT

Cooper v Clay

One of the all-time British heavyweight boxers, Henry Cooper gained most respect for his non-title fight with Cassius Clay on 18 June 1963 at Wembley Stadium.

Clay, already being hailed as a future world champion, was unbeaten in 18 fights while Cooper had won 12 out of his last 13. There were few who believed Cooper could end the brash American's progress but with his amazing punching power – especially a vicious left hook, known as 'Enery's 'Ammer', that had become his calling card – there was always the possibility of an upset.

Clay, soon to change his name to Muhammad Ali, was on the receiving end of 'Enery's 'Ammer' in the fourth round. He hit the canvas but was saved by the bell. Clay was so dazed that it is alleged that his trainer Angelo Dundee cut his glove, so gaining him vital recovery time while a replacement was brought from the dressing room, and the debate rages to this day. (The rules were changed in the aftermath of this fight so that a spare pair of gloves must be kept in the boxer's corner.)

As it was, the cut that Clay had inflicted on Cooper's left eye in the Third Round gave the referee sufficient cause for concern that he stopped the fight in the Fifth. This was Cooper's best chance to defeat Clay, who went on to become World Champion after knocking out Sonny Liston the following year.

Cooper, born 3 May 1934, did meet Ali again in the ring, this time in a title fight in 1966 but the American was now wary and kept his distance. The end result was the same, with the fight being stopped in the Sixth Round after Cooper had once again been cut.

Following his retirement, Cooper became a TV personality advertising Brut aftershave and in 2000 became the first boxer to be knighted.

Below: Cassius Clay and Henry Cooper shake hands after Clay's victory in a non-title fight at Wembley. Cooper suffered a bad gash under his left eye in the fight.

Restricted overs were introduced into English county cricket to produce a result

In a bid to bring more excitement into cricket and attract more spectators in the face of dwindling attendances, the 1963 English cricket season saw the introduction of limited overs matches. Known as one-day cricket, it was believed that if a match were played to a conclusion in a single day with an agreed number of overs – usually 50 – this would persuade the punters to part with their hard-earned money.

The idea was so successful that it was adopted by the international scene in 1971 when a match was played on the fifth day of a rained-off Test on England's tour of Australia. Hence one-day internationals (ODIs) were born – although there is always a reserve day if the weather proves unsuitable – and they are still a huge success today. This also led to the creation of a World Cup, the first being held in England in 1975 and won by the West Indies.

Spurs win Cup Winners' Cup

Having beaten Burnley in the 1962 FA Cup Final, Tottenham Hotspur thereby qualified for the following season's European Cup Winners' Cup. As they had only lost to Benfica 4-3 on aggregate in the 1961-62 European Cup semi-final, their fans knew they had the quality to compete with the best in Europe.

Their first match at the end of October saw them play host to Glasgow Rangers and the home side eased into a 5-2 first-leg advantage with John White scoring twice (he would be killed the following year after being struck by lightning on a golf course). The return leg was not until mid-December but a brace from Bobby Smith and one from Jimmy Greaves ensured their passage into the quarter-finals with an 8-4 aggregate victory.

Below: Leicestershire against Surrey at the Oval.

REMEMBER THE SIXTIES

Slovan Bratislava proved tougher opponents away than at home with Spurs losing the first leg 2-0 but then thrashing the Czechs 6-0 at White Hart Lane, Greaves's two goals helping to set up a Semi-Final meeting with OFK Belgrade.

A stunning 2-1 victory in Belgrade set the scene for a packed White Hart Lane and the fans did not go home disappointed as Cliff Jones, Dave Mackay and Smith each scored in the 3-1 victory that took Spurs through to their first ever European Final.

Their opponents on 15 May in Rotterdam were Spanish giants and holders Atletico Madrid yet Spurs gave them no chance. Greaves converted a Jones cross after 15 minutes to open the scoring and White netted a

second soon after. Madrid managed to get back into the match as the second half began when Enrique Collar scored from the penalty spot after Ron Henry had handled a goal-bound shot.

Dyson restored their two-goal cushion before Greaves netted his 44th goal of the season to dispel any fears that the Cup would not be going to White Hart Lane. With a second goal from Dyson rounding the match off, Spurs finished 5-1 winners and became the first British club to win a European trophy.

Below: Tottenham Hotspur proudly display the FA Cup after defeating Burnley in the final. This enabled them to qualify for the European Cup Winners' Cup, which they went on to win.

1960 1961 1962 **1963** 1964 1965 1966 1967 1968 1969

1960 1961 1962 1963 1964 1965 1966 1967 1968 1969

POLITICS & CURRENT AFFAIRS

The Profumo Affair

The early 1960s saw the beginning of sexual liberation in Britain, and it could be argued that John Profumo – War Minister in Harold Macmillan's Conservative

During 1963 it emerged that there had been naughty goings-on at Cliveden, the Maidenhead home of Lord Astor. When the full story emerged, it transpired that Profumo had been having a steamy affair with one Christine Keeler, who in turn had also had an affair with a Soviet naval attaché called Eugene Ivanov. There had also been some very strange parties at the home of society osteopath Stephen Ward, and the public was soon treated to a variety of lurid tales involving Ward, another showgirl called Mandy Rice-Davies, and a 'prominent figure' known as the 'Man in the Mask', who apparently served meals to guests at Ward's parties in the nude – before eating his own meal from a dog's bowl. Rumour had it that he was another government minister, although this was never proved.

Profumo was probably on the margins of many of these goings-on but, apart from the obvious sex scandal itself, there were two things that led to his downfall. Firstly, it

government – started it all. Profumo was a well-liked politician, educated at Harrow and Oxford, and a rising star within the Conservative Party. Government ministers do well not to get involved with showgirls, however, and Profumo's sparkling political career was soon to be cut short.

Above and Below: English Conservative politician John Profumo as War Minister and Mandy Rice-Davies with Christine Keeler.

seemed likely that Mr Ivanov was a spy, and that national security had been compromised. Secondly, Profumo lied to parliament. In a statement, he said: 'Miss Keeler and I were on friendly terms. There was no impropriety whatsoever in my acquaintanceship with Miss Keeler.'

Profumo was forced to resign, claiming 'deep remorse' about the fact that he had lied. Harold Macmillan also resigned soon afterwards. Profumo immersed himself in charity work, and in 1975 was awarded the CBE. He died in 2006, aged 91.

JFK assassinated

Just a few months after John Fitzgerald Kennedy made his famous 'Ich bin ein Berliner' speech in support of West Germany, the thirty-fifth President of the United States was gunned down in Dallas, Texas. Kennedy was the fourth American president to be assassinated, and the eighth to die in office. He met his end in a Lincoln Continental limousine at 12.30pm on Friday 22 November 1963, while visiting the city on a mission to raise funds and support for the 1964 presidential election.

The president was young and popular (at least amongst supporters of the Democratic Party) and most had difficulty in believing that such a tragedy had really

Above: President John F Kennedy and his wife Jacqueline Kennedy ride with secret agents in an open car motorcade shortly before he was assassinated.

1960 1961 1962 **1963** 1964 1965 1966 1967 1968 1969

happened. Security had been tight, but not tight enough. The idea of a world leader travelling in an open car would seem incredible today, but Kennedy was there to be shot at, from the Texas School Book Depository in nearby Dealey Plaza, some 20 metres away. He was rushed to the Parkland Memorial Hospital, but was declared dead upon arrival. Although the event was not recorded by television or film crews, the amateur footage of Kennedy's last moments later became famous throughout the world. People wept openly in the street.

There have been dozens of theories concerning the assassination. Lee Harvey Oswald, who was arrested for the killing, but was himself murdered by Jack Ruby before he could be brought to trial, claimed he had been set up, and to this day nobody really knows how the president, together with Texas Governor Connally (who survived) came to be shot. But shot he was, and vice-president Lyndon Baines Johnson was later that day filmed on board the president's plane, taking the presidential oath. JFK's widow, Jackie, was at his side.

The Great Train Robbery

On 8 August 1963 a Royal Mail train travelling from Glasgow to London was brought to a halt near the village of Linslade in Buckinghamshire. This was the start of the Great Train Robbery, which netted its participants £2.3 million – equal to about £40 million today. Fifteen robbers took part, the most infamous being Ronnie Biggs, Charlie Wilson and Buster Edwards, and 13 were

Below: Lee Harvey Oswald alleged assassin of John F Kennedy detained by a police officer, November 1963.

eventually caught. The driver, Jack Mills, was struck with an iron bar during the robbery, and never completely recovered.

Buster Edwards fled to Mexico after the robbery, but gave himself up after three years. He ended his days selling flowers outside Waterloo Station. Charlie Wilson and Ronnie Biggs were captured, but escaped from prison. Wilson was eventually traced in Canada, and was brought back to Britain, but Biggs led the high life in Brazil for many years, becoming a kind of national anti-hero. Having suffered several strokes, he gave himself up to the British authorities in 2001.

1960 1961 1962 **1963** 1964 1965 1966 1967 1968 1969

Above and below: Investigators examine the Royal Mail train involved in the 'Great Train Robbery' and three of the suspects arrested in connection with the robbery leaving Linslade court with blankets over their heads.

1969 1968 1967 1966 1965 **1964** 1963 1962 1961 1960

1964

FASHION, CULTURE & ENTERTAINMENT

My Fair Lady

In 1964, director George Cukor released his film musical adaptation of George Bernard Shaw's 1912 play *Pygmalion*. The romantic musical from Warner Brothers was their most expensive film at the time, costing around $17 million, mainly because they had to pay $5.5 million for the rights to Shaw's Broadway hit.

Due to its clever lyrics, melodic songs, stunning costumes and lavish sets along with great actors in leading roles, including, Audrey Hepburn as Eliza Doolittle and Rex Harrison as Professor Henry Higgins, the film became one of the top five films of 1964.

The story centres around Higgins's wager with Colonel Pickering that he can take an unrefined Cockney flower girl and teach her to speak properly within six months. The then, little-known, Julie Andrews, who was successfully playing the flower girl on Broadway (which ran from 1956 to 1962) was overlooked for the part of Eliza when producer Jack Warner preferred Hepburn even though she could not sing and her vocals were dubbed by Marnie Nixon.

While Eliza benefits from elocution lessons with Higgins, her unrepentant, drunken father appears throughout the film for handouts. During an

Above: The mixing desk at an early 'Top of the Pops'.
Below: Audrey Hepburn and Rex Harrison, stars of the film 'My Fair Lady'.

embarrassing first appearance at the opening day of Ascot Races, Eliza catches the eye of Freddy Eynsford-Hill. Eliza's snobbish and arrogant teacher takes all the credit for her transformation into a lady and she angrily leaves him for Freddy. Higgins realises he is unable to live without Eliza and sets out to win her back.

Top of the Pops

Arguably the best known television music show of its time, *Top Of The Pops* was launched by the BBC on 1 January 1964. Originally commissioned for six shows, it was transmitted from a converted church in Manchester.

Today, there have been more than 2,000 editions of the show with presenters such as Tony Blackburn, Noel Edmunds, Alan Freeman, Simon Bates and Richard Bacon, not to mention 'golden oldies' David Jacobs and Pete Murray.

The original format has stayed the same for over 40 years and provides a weekly snapshot of what's popular in the Top 40 chart. Each show always ends with that week's Number 1 record.

Sir Jimmy Savile, DJ and television presenter introduced the first show on a Wednesday evening with opening band the Rolling Stones playing 'I Wanna Be Your Man', then at Number 13 in the charts. Dusty Springfield sang 'I Only Want To Be

With You' followed by the Dave Clark Five and 'Glad All Over', the Hollies with 'Stay' and 'The Hippy Hippy Shake', performed by the Swinging Blue Jeans. There were also filmed performances by Freddie and the Dreamers and Cliff Richard and the Shadows. The week's Number 1 was 'I Want To Hold Your Hand' by the Beatles.

Denise Sampey spun the records for the first few programmes and was then replaced by model Samantha Juste. Dance groups Pan's People and Legs & Co were introduced in the 1970s, gyrating suggestively when solo artists and bands were not available to appear on the show.

Today, *Top of the Pops*, known as *TOTP*, boasts a dedicated website where fans can get the latest chart information, read interviews with current artists, catch up with gossip and videos, including clips from the latest shows. *TOTP* also has the highest selling music magazine in the UK.

Above: The Hollies who were regulars on 'Top of the Pops', posing with their guitars.

1960 1961 1962 1963 **1964** 1965 1966 1967 1968 1969

With the programme shunted to a Sunday-night BBC2 slot and it not being as influential as it was in its heyday, the BBC made the decision to end its 42-year run in 2006.

Habitat

Terence Conran opened his first Habitat household furnishing store at 77 Fulham Road, London, in May 1964, bringing innovation and affordable design to the UK. Much of the furniture was imported from Europe, and the people of London were introduced to a range of French cookware. Today there are more than 70 stores in the UK, France, Germany and Spain and other countries such as Belgium, Cyprus, Iceland and Thailand operate franchises.

Conran's first designs were the Summa range, which he displayed against a backdrop of quarry tiled floors, whitewashed brick walls and white wooden-slatted ceilings. Spotlights were used to create a feeling of space while also focusing the customer's attention on the product. Conran thought that initial success

came from selling cheap pasta storage jars at a time when the market for dried pasta took off in the UK. The other innovative idea which helped Habitat's success was the publication of a catalogue that showed the store's products in an idealised interior, creating the impression that the customer was buying into a lifestyle.

John Lennon, George Harrison and Julie Christie all bought products from Habitat, as did clothes designer Mary Quant who also designed staff outfits. Today, Habitat is part of the IKANO Group.

First Scalextric World Championships

Scalextric model racing cars were introduced to the market in 1952 by the company Minimodels. Invented by a Mr B Francis, they were a range of metal-bodied

Above: *Jim Clark sitting in his Lotus – he helped promote Scalextric.*
Below: *Mary Quant who designed the staff uniforms for Habitat.*

cars containing a unique clockwork motor, released under the trademark Scalex.

However popularity of the mini-models waned around 1956 and Francis began searching for new ways to update the product. He redesigned them to include an electric motor, devising a rubber-based road surface with parallel grooves in which metal rails carried an electric current enabling the cars to motor around the track.

Developments in the late Fifties led to a new product, Scalextric, being launched at the Harrogate Toy Fair in January 1957. Success was immediate and further developments by 1964 led to the slogan 'the most complete model motor racing system in the world...' The appeal of the racing cars really took off when Formula 1 driver Jim Clark promoted the product and the first Scalextric World Championship was staged in London.

Topless swimsuit

Women were liberated in 1964 by designer Rudi Gernreich, a free spirit in the fashion world, who designed the controversial topless swimsuit. The swimsuit, also known as a monokini, exposed breasts for the first time in commercial fashion.

Gernreich, a gay activist, had fled Austria and the Nazis aged 16 and settled in the US initially working as a dancer. He moved into fashion design, through an interest in textiles. The French and Italian couture designers of the time were considered prim and stuffy by the young, and Gernreich's designs were a welcome change. As a top designer he produced innovative and sometimes controversial designs with simple lines and modern styles.

Model Peggy Moffitt, who worked extensively with Gernreich, modelled the first topless swimsuit, making international headlines. The swimsuit soon led to the pubikini (leaving a window so that the woman's pubic hair was exposed) the topless dress and the revolutionary no-bra bra which changed the way clothes fitted women. It produced a 'natural' look which Gernreich stated, freed women from padding and boning. Gernreich also designed the thong bikini and was the first designer to use vinyl and plastic in clothes.

1960 1961 1962 1963 **1964** 1965 1966 1967 1968 1969

Below: Peggy Moffitt who caused a sensation when she modelled the first topless swimsuit.

MUSIC

March

The Dave Clark Five were the first British beat group to undertake a full-scale North American tour. Though 'Glad All Over', their recent UK chart-topper, had soared into the US Top 20, the Five's reception at New York's John F Kennedy Airport – reported on BBC television's

Nine O'Clock News – was muted by comparison to the Beatles' tumultuous touch-down a few weeks earlier for a handful of shows and, like the Five, to appear on the nationally-networked *Ed Sullivan Show*.

By summer, the Kinks too were high in the Hot 100, and the Animals became the second UK beat group after the Beatles to top the list – with an edited version of 'The House Of The Rising Sun' – following it up with a messianic descent on New York in September where they were provided with a chauffeured Mustang convertible each for transport to the hotel. 'Britain hasn't been so influential in American affairs since 1775,' read

a *Billboard* editorial as fascination with all things pop from our sceptred isle peaked in the autumn week when two-thirds of the Hot 100 was British in origin.

Most of the UK's major acts – and a few minor ones – succeeded to varying degrees during what has passed into myth as the 'British Invasion'. Some would be far bigger over there than they ever were at home – notably the Dave Clark Five, who took Uncle Sam for every cent they could get via relentless bi-annual treks across the sub-continent and scheduling a gap as little as six weeks between catchpenny albums.

Other Limeys encroached on the New World via pop-associated professions. These included DJ John Peel, who was engaged as 'Beatle expert'

Above: *The Dave Clark Five wearing matching white suits and paisley shirts.*
Below: *The Kinks pose for a promotional photo.*

retrospectively – if you believe tabloid archives – as portentous in microcosm as the Anglo-Saxon Chronicle's entry for 787 AD about 'three ships of the Northmen' attacking Weymouth Bay, and precipitating further-reaching Viking ravages that would trouble the realm over the next three centuries.

In truth, enmity between the two tribes was never as virulent as newshounds under the editorial lash made out. In provinces where the distance to Swinging London was measurable in years as much as miles, would-be Mods – dandified riders of motor-scooters – and Rockers – perpetually leather-jacketed

1964

by a Dallas radio network. Clothes designer Mary Quant and top models Jean Shrimpton and Twiggy also 'arrived' in the States in 1964. In the same mini-skirted league, George Harrison's fiancée, Pattie Boyd was commissioned by *Sixteen* magazine to pen a regular 'Letter From London', while Shrimpton's sister Chrissie was likewise engaged to report for its sister US publication, *Mod*, on the activities of London's in-crowd in her capacity as Mick Jagger's girlfriend.

March

The UK media was full of families on the beaches of Clacton-on-Sea, Essex cowering as Mods and Rockers fought their first major battle. This instance of scuffles, stonings and deckchair-hurling by the two principal factions in mid-1960s British youth culture, seems

Above: Twiggy wearing a red tasselled mini dress with matching boots.
Below: Jean Shrimpton, the model.

1969 1968 1967 1966 1965 1964 1963 1962 1961 1960

bikers – would simply congregate at opposite ends of a cafe, though there were still ructions at dances and at the predetermined invasions of seaside resorts during bank holiday weekends. 'It wasn't so much violence as hordes of young people running around and looking for the excitement that others were committing, expounded John Albon, an 18-year-old in 1964. 'We were like a huge mobile audience though in fact we were the main act. There were fights, but they were kind of hit-and-run. Nevertheless, the tradition of police manning-up for public holidays continued to the mid-1960s.'

By then, Mod had reached the masses, principally through pirate radio and *Ready Steady Go*, ITV's weekly pop series. London-type boutiques sprang up in other cities and the bigger towns, and it was possible to be merely a few steps behind the capital with paper-round-

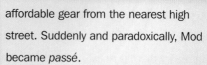

affordable gear from the nearest high street. Suddenly and paradoxically, Mod became *passé*.

By way of a postscript, one of the participants in the Clacton conflict was a certain David Cook, later 1970s pop star David Essex. En route, his malfunctioning scooter had come to a halt, 'leaving me to run the risk of being pummelled by passing Rockers'.

July

'To retain the attention of the public,' the Who's Pete Townshend was to pontificate, 'every pop star has to make

Above: Armed guards carry canisters with prints of the film, 'A Hard Day's Night' past screaming fans.
Below: David Essex, the mod.

Britain's hit parade for weeks, necessitating the avoidance of such revenue-draining clashes in future.

October

In the Stratford-on-Avon by-election, caused by the resignation of the minister who lent his name to the Profumo Scandal, Screaming Lord Sutch stood as a Parliamentary candidate in the first of many attempts to gain political office over the decades that preceded his death in 1999. Predictably, his National Teenage (later, Monster Raving Loony) Party lost its deposit. Yet the publicity amassed by his media sideshow helped sustain what was, on its own terms, the triumphant professional career of the most illustrious English rock icon who never had a hit.

Gradually, this came to have as great a bearing on Sutch's life as pop via singles like 'Rock The Election'

the transition to films. It's the only way to last.' *A Hard Day's Night*, the Beatles' first – and most attractive – venture into the movies was produced by Walter Shenson, whose past had included 1962's *A Band Of Thieves*, a showcase for the 'economic' thespian abilities of Acker Bilk's Paramount Jazz Band. Yet, if the Fab Four flick was also a neo-musical about happy-go-lucky funsters, a bluff lyricism pervaded a not completely unrealistic fictionalisation of the group's eventful preparation for a television show. Also, John, Paul, George and Ringo were not required 'to other be'. That was left to a high calibre of supporting actors.

Its soundtrack album amassed over a million advance orders, and the title track single vied with the Rolling Stones' 'It's All Over Now' for the top slot in

Below: Leader and founder of the National Teenage party David Sutch.

1960 1961 1962 1963 **1964** 1965 1966 1967 1968 1969

and 1991's 'Number 10 Or Bust'. Nonetheless, even though he played it mostly for laughs, he often beat so-called 'serious' contenders and remains the country's longest-serving political leader. Moreover, many of his proposals – among them votes at 18, the legalisation of commercial radio and passports for pets – proved surprisingly prophetic.

November

Detroit's Tamla Motown label scored its maiden UK chart-topper in November 1964 with 'Baby Love' by the Supremes. Florence Ballard, Diane Earl – who was to adopt the stage name Diana Ross – and Mary Wilson had emerged from a black vocal quartet, the Primettes, formed in 1959. Signed by Motown the following year,

their first singles swallowed dust behind such as Barrett Strong's 'Money', 'Please Mr. Postman' by the Marvelettes and others manoeuvred by the company into the US Hot 100.

In 1964, however, linking the house songwriting team of Lamont Dozier and Brian and Eddie Holland spawned a US Top 30 entry with 'When The Lovelight Starts Shining Through His Eyes.' While the 'Run Run Run' follow-up flopped, paradise was regained with 'Where Did Our Love Go', the international million-seller that paved the way for 'Baby Love'.

Now established as permanent lead singer, Ross was well-placed for solo stardom, while Ballard, who had fronted the trio originally, was to die in poverty in 1976.

Above: The Supremes with Diana Ross on the right.

SPORT

Tokyo Olympics

The first ever Olympic Games to be held in Asia took place in Tokyo in 1964, 24 years after the Japanese wartime government had forced their Olympic Committee to resign as hosts after they had last been awarded the honour. A staggering $3 billion was spent preparing the city and its venues and the organisers would have been ecstatic with the record-breaking Games that followed.

Britain had their most successful Games since 1908, finishing with a tally of four gold, 12 silver and 2 bronze medals. Ken Matthews continued Britain's success in the walking events, claiming gold in the 20 kilometre walk with a record time of one hour 29 minutes and 34 seconds.

There was a double in the long jump, with Welsh school teacher Lynn Davies jumping 8.07 metres to

become the first British man to hold a field event title. Mary Rand also registered a first, as her 6.76 metres jump meant she was the first British woman to win a gold medal and break the world record.

Middle-distance runner Ann Packer claimed Britain's fourth gold with a world record time giving her an 800 metres gold medal to go with the silver she had won in the 400 metres.

Other notable results saw Ethiopia's Abebe Bikila become the first runner to retain his marathon title when he finished four minutes ahead of his nearest rival...and this just an amazing five weeks after he had had his appendix removed. New Zealander Peter Snell became only the second man (after Albert Hill in 1920)

Above: Mary Rand in action during the long jump at the Olympic Games.
Below: Ken Matthews, supported by his wife Sheila after winning the 20 kilometre walk at the Tokyo Olympics.

1960 1961 1962 1963 1964 1965 1966 1967 1968 1969

Guards Captain Robin Dixon won the two-man bobsled event at the 1964 Winter Olympics to claim their country's first gold medal for 12 years.

The British team had broken a bolt that attached the runners to the shell of their bobsled after the first run, but Italian Eugenio Monti – in true Olympic spirit – lent them one from his sled and eventually finished third.

Innsbruck, hosting the Games for the first time, saw rather less snow than usual, enjoying spring-like temperatures both before and during the Games. The Austrian military came to the rescue, however, transporting over 50,000 cubic metres of snow to the courses.

to win both the 800 and 1,500 metres titles. Soviet gymnast Larissa Latynina won six medals for the third Olympics in a row with two golds, two silvers and two bronzes in the team and individual disciplines. American Don Schollander, just 18, became the first swimmer to win four events in one Games when he claimed two individual and two relay gold medals.

British two-man bobsled team win gold at Innsbruck Winter Olympics

For a country that does not see much snow and has not got its own bobsleigh run, it was a remarkable achievement when British duo Tony Nash and Grenadier

Above: Peter Snell winning the 800 metres final.
Below: Larissa Latynina in action during the women's compulsory exercises at the Tokyo Olympics.

The Games had been marred by the death of two athletes less than a week before the opening ceremony. British luger Kazimierz Kay-Skyszpeski and Australian downhill skier Ross Milne were killed taking practice runs in anticipation of the competition.

West Ham and Preston contest epic FA Cup Final

It is not very often that a lower division side causes an upset in the FA Cup Final but it almost happened in 1964. West Ham United were entering their halcyon days of the mid-1960s when players such as Bobby Moore, Martin Peters and Geoff Hurst graced the Upton Park turf.

Ron Greenwood had assembled a quality side that claimed their first FA Cup trophy this year, went on to win the European Cup Winners' Cup the following season and finished as runners-up in the 1966 League Cup Final.

Preston North End, on the other hand, were entering a period of huge disappointment. They had been relegated from the First Division at the end of 1960-61

and by 1970 would be in the third tier for the first time in their history.

The Hammers therefore arrived at Wembley – the first time they had reached the FA Cup Final since losing 2-0 to Bolton Wanderers in 1923 – as the pre-match favourites but it was Second Division Preston who settled quickest, with teenager Howard Kendall becoming the youngest player ever to appear in the showpiece.

Within ten minutes, North End had upset the formbooks when West Ham keeper Jim Standen failed to hold an Alex Dawson shot which Doug Holden followed up to score. The lead did not last long, however, John Sissons quickly restoring parity, but the Lilywhites regained their advantage shortly before half-time with a Dawson header.

Hurst equalised in the second half to set up a thrilling finish as West Ham looked to capitalise on their domination but Preston came back into the game the more the half went on.

1960 1961 1962 1963 **1964** 1965 1966 1967 1968 1969

Above: Tony Nash (pilot) and Robin Dixon win a gold medal for Britain in the bobsleigh race.
Below: West Ham United captain Bobby Moore raises the FA Cup after his team's victory over Preston North End.

It was West Ham who secured a last-gasp winner when Hurst set off towards his opponent's goal as the clock ticked past 90 minutes. The ball found its way to Peter Brabrook who crossed for Ronnie Boyce to head home.

POLITICS & CURRENT AFFAIRS

Harold Wilson – Prime Minister

Born in Huddersfield in 1916, Harold Wilson was the son of an industrial chemist. Although he learned to present himself as a man of the people, he was in fact an intellectual with a first class brain. After Jesus College, Oxford, he became a civil servant, before entering Parliament in 1945 as one of its youngest members. Wilson suffered one or two setbacks, but soon learned how to climb the greasy pole. His colleagues in the Labour Party did not always trust him but, when their leader Hugh Gaitskell died unexpectedly in 1963, Wilson managed to get himself elected as party leader.

The Conservatives were in decline. Lord Home had given up his title in 1963 to succeed Harold Macmillan as Prime Minister, and his Lordship, now to be known as Sir Alec Douglas-Home, was seen as the last of a

Above: West Ham parade the FA Cup on an open-top bus through the streets of London.

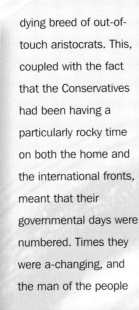

dying breed of out-of-touch aristocrats. This, coupled with the fact that the Conservatives had been having a particularly rocky time on both the home and the international fronts, meant that their governmental days were numbered. Times they were a-changing, and the man of the people was to have his day. On 15 October 1964 the voters went to the polls, and they elected a Labour government with an overall majority of just four seats – the smallest margin of victory for more than a hundred years.

Harold and his wife Mary, who wrote poetry and never quite got used to the idea of being a prime minister's wife, duly moved into number 10 Downing Street. Wilson, who had described Douglas-Home as 'a scion of the effete establishment' declared that Britain would be transformed after '13 wasted years under the Tories'. He was to undergo many difficulties, but in 1964 he set about the task of creating a fairer Britain.

Below: Harold Wilson in the Cabinet Room at Number Ten Downing Street.

1960 1961 1962 1963 **1964** 1965 1966 1967 1968 1969

Brezhnev ousts Khrushchev

By the early 1960s, Nikita Khrushchev was coming towards the end of his reign as Premier of the Soviet Union. According to many of his Party colleagues he was beginning to go soft on the West, largely giving in over the Cuban missile crisis, and speaking as he sometimes did of 'peaceful co-existence'. He was also beginning to show signs of instability. His outbursts were becoming an embarrassment, and his banging of a shoe on the table at a 1960 United Nations conference had not done a lot for his image as a statesman. Accordingly, by 1963, a plot to have him removed was well and truly afoot.

Leonid Ilyich Brezhnev had been a protégé of Khrushchev. Educated in land management, and later as a metallurgist, he had joined the Communist Party Youth Organisation in 1923 and become a full member of the party in 1931. He had known little but Stalinism, and he was fully committed to Stalin's policies. By

TUESDAY • • • •

SUN

SEPTEMBER 15 1964   THREEPENCE   No. 1

THE INDEPENDENT DAILY NEWSPAPER

GOO
YES,
A NE

Election race is on

By TREVOR WILLIAMS, Political Reporter

THEY'RE OFF in the General Election stakes. Today the starting tape goes up for 1,600 men and women in the race for 630 seats in the next House of Commons.

The election date will be made known officially at about 4 pm. today from 10. Downing Street. October 15 can be regarded

1950 he was a deputy of the Supreme Soviet, and his rise to power was well and truly underway. During the 1950s he at first backed Khrushchev in his struggle against the old guard leadership, but being a Soviet politician he doubtless already had his eye on the main chance.

Brezhnev became Secretary of the Central Committee, and was thus first in line to succeed Khrushchev as First Secretary of the Communist Party when the time came. The Soviet Union was having big problems,

Below: Leonid Ilyich Brezhnev.

MORNING!
'S TIME FOR
NEWSPAPER

THE British public believe it is time for a new newspaper, born of the age we live in. That is why the SUN rises brightly today.

Here it is—Number One issue of the first new popular daily in this country for 34 years. What does this newspaper stand for? What is its sense of purpose? What is it all about?

★ The Sun is politically free. It will not automatically support or censure any party or any Government.

★ It is an independent paper designed to serve and inform all those whose lives are changing, improving, expanding in these hurrying years.

★ We welcome the age of automation, electronics, computers. We will campaign for the rapid modernisation of Britain—regardless of the vested interests of managements or workers. But we will crusade against any Government which drives the evolution forward without farsighted schemes for retraining, and generous compensation where unemployment arises.

★ The Sun is a newspaper with a social conscience. A radical paper, ready to praise or criticise without precon-

Today's weather

serious daily newspaper aimed at working-class men and women. It did well until it ran into financial problems in 1929, whereupon it was taken over by Odhams Press. It then flourished once more.

The *Daily Herald* was a well written and informative newspaper, and it was a virtual organ of the Labour Party for many years. Circulation figures dropped after a time however, and in 1964 the paper was re-launched as *The Sun*. At first it was not unlike its predecessor, but then Rupert Murdoch's News International group took it over and changed it forever. The striking printers of 1911 would have some difficulty in recognising their paper today.

especially on the agricultural front, and so Brezhnev became involved in a plot to ensure Khrushchev's downfall. In 1964, Khrushchev was removed from power while he was on holiday, and Brezhnev became the effective leader of the Soviet Union. Khrushchev was placed under house arrest for seven years, dying in 1971. Brezhnev proved to be less of a reformer than his predecessor, and the Cold War continued.

The Sun shines forth

In January 1911 publication of the *Daily Herald* commenced in support of the London printing unions which were striking over poor pay and conditions. The paper was extremely successful, and was soon transformed into a

Above and below: The front page of the first edition of the Sun newspaper and the Sun editorial offices.

1960 1961 1962 1963 1964 1965 1966 1967 1968 1969

1965

FASHION, CULTURE & ENTERTAINMENT

Stan Laurel dies

After suffering a heart attack, Stan Laurel died on 23 February 1965 and the world lost a brilliant comic actor. He was buried at Forest Lawn, Hollywood Hills Cemetery in Los Angeles.

Born into a theatrical family in June 1890 in Ulverston, Cumbria, Arthur Stanley Jefferson (Laurel's real name) enjoyed a happy childhood spending much time with his grandmother while his father was busy running a number of theatres. He had a natural affinity with the theatre and in 1910 joined a troupe of actors which included Charlie Chaplin. Stan was often understudy to Chaplin. The troupe toured America and, between 1916 and 1918, Stan was to meet some of his lifelong friends, including Mae Dahlberg who suggested he adopt the stage name Laurel. *Nuts in May*, Stan's first film saw Universal offer him a contract.

Mae's temperament and interfering in Stan's career was hindering him and in 1925 Mae was offered a cash settlement and one-way ticket to her native Australia by Joe Rock. Stan went on to join Hal Roach's studio, where he intended to work primarily as a writer and director. But fate stepped in and he was in front of the camera with another Hal Roach employee, Oliver Hardy. It was immediately obvious that the two men had a natural comic chemistry and the result was one of the most successful pairings in cinema history.

Laurel and Hardy made more than 50 films together during the 1930s and early 1940s. Their 1932 *The Music Box* won the Oscar for Best Short Subject. Although Stan Laurel survived Oliver Hardy, who died of

a stroke in 1957, by eight years, he was unable to go to the funeral due to his own ill health. Friends of Laurel said he never fully recovered from his friend's death.

Mary Poppins

In 1965, *Mary Poppins*, the musical film version by Walt Disney won five Oscars – the highest number ever for a Disney musical – a British Academy award and a Golden Globe. Based on the children's books by PL Travers, which were illustrated by Mary Shepard, the film stars

Above: Oliver Hardy (left) and his partner Stan Laurel on a pair of wooden horses.

Julie Andrews as the English nanny and Dick Van Dyke as a Cockney chimney sweep.

The film centres on the Banks family who live at Number 17, Cherry Tree Lane, London and the relationship that the children – Jane and Michael – have with their nanny. Jane and Michael write an advertisement for a new nanny when their previous, stuffy nanny has had more than enough of their antics. They ask for a nanny with 'a cheery disposition, rosy cheeks and no warts', but get more than they bargained for when Mary Poppins provides them with many magical diversions.

production of Mary Poppins. Andrews won the Academy Award for Best Actress in a Leading Role.

The film also won Best Music Score (by Richard M Sherman), Best Music Song 'for Chim, Chim, Chiree',

Nominated for 13 Academy Awards, a record for a movie musical, the film is a mixture of live action and clever animation and has a host of memorable songs including 'Supercalifragilisticexpialidocious'.

Despite her success in the Broadway production of My Fair Lady, Julie Andrews was rejected by Jack Warner, for not being photogenic enough for the part of Eliza Doolittle in the film version that was eventually to star Audrey Hepburn and Rex Harrison. Walt Disney didn't agree with Warner and cast her to star in his

85

Above: David Tomlinson (Mr Banks) poses behind a gilt picture frame in a promo for 'Mary Poppins'.
Below: Julie Andrews, with the Academy Award she won for her role in 'Mary Poppins'.

1960 1961 1962 1963 1964 1965 1966 1967 1968 1969

Robert B Sherman, Best Effects (Peter Ellenshaw) and Best Film Editing (Cotton Warburton). Julie Andrews also went on to win the BAFTA award for Most Promising Newcomer and the Golden Globe for Best Motion Picture Actress in a Musical/Comedy.

Thunderbirds

The first episode of innovative children's TV show *Thunderbirds*, 'Trapped in the Sky,' was aired on television on 2 October 1965. The concept for the 'super-marionation' was the brainchild of producer Gerry Anderson who, while listening to the radio, heard coverage of a mining disaster in Germany. It sparked an idea for a dedicated rescue team equipped with highly advanced equipment.

Gerry and Sylvia Anderson kept to a simple formula where secret organisation International Rescue is dedicated to saving lives. It was ingenious as episodes are set in an unknown location which meant that the series was timeless, was free from politics and had international appeal.

Millionaire ex-astronaut Jeff Tracy heads International Rescue which carries out daring missions using a range of highly developed Thunderbird aircraft which are launched from a secret island base. Tracy's five sons, all named after the first US astronauts in space, pilot the aircraft.

Despite worldwide success, the programme's inability to attract a deal with a US network meant the series was cancelled early in its second season.

Below: The cast of puppets from 'Thunderbirds'.

chilled-out feel it was renowned for during its modernism days. It has its own dedicated website and newsletter, where visitors can find out everything from where to shop and where to eat to forthcoming events.

Plastic dress

It was innovative designer Rudi Gernreich who first experimented with vinyl and plastic as materials for clothes. However, it was John Bates, probably best remembered for his Mod designs for actress Diana Rigg of *The Avengers*, who first came up with the plastic dress.

French couturier Pierre Cardin had also hit on the more relaxed Mod styles and became known for his 'Space Age' look. But Bates's dress, modelled by Twiggy in 1965, was to inspire him to create his most famous design, the A-line dress with the midriff cut out and replaced by sheer netting. It was voted Dress of the Year, 1965.

Carnaby Street

Just east of Regent Street, off Great Marlborough Street at the heart of London's Soho, lies Carnaby Street. It is named after Karnaby House, a large building located east of the street which was built in 1683. It's not known where the building got its name, but the actual street was probably laid out sometime in 1685 or 1686 as it first appears in rate books in 1687. By 1690 the entire street was lined with small houses.

During the mid-1960s Carnaby Street became synonymous with Mod fashion and became popular when many independent music shops, fashion boutiques and designers such as Mary Quant had shops there. *Time Magazine* described it at the time as the 'swinging city'.

Pedestrian-friendly Carnaby Street is still popular today with its vibrant atmosphere, good shops and restaurants. After many years of neglect following its popularity in the 1960s, Carnaby Street is once again gaining a reputation as a hot spot for cutting edge fashion. Despite its colourful edge, it has retained the

1960 1961 1962 1963 1964 **1965** 1966 1967 1968 1969

Above: Young shoppers walking along Carnaby Street.
Below: Twiggy modelling a transparent plastic halterneck dress.

John Bates has remained largely unappreciated for his contribution to the innovation and creativity of the London fashion scene. He set up 28 Jean Varon boutiques within UK department stores and was one of the first designers along with Mary Quant to raise hemlines. The key to his success was recognition of the youth market and his ability to cater for it.

MUSIC

January

The yo-yo progression of the Who's first single, 'I Can't Explain', to the upper reaches of the Top 20 was assisted by a long weekly residency at central London's prestigious Marquee – with posters promising 'Maximum R&B' – and an astonishing debut on ITV's *Ready Steady Go!* in which drummer Keith Moon was as prominent visually as vocalist Roger

Daltrey. Yet to come was the group's practice of closing the act by smashing up their equipment amid smoke bombs, flashing lights and feedback.

'I Can't Explain' – composed by guitarist Pete Townshend – absorbed salient points of the Kinks' riff-based smashes that began with the previous summer's

'You Really Got Me'. With Daltrey, Townshend was to write the 'Anyway Anyhow Anywhere' follow-up, which was a lesser hit, but a hit all the same in summer 1965. Its explosive instrumental break was heard over *Ready Steady Go!*'s opening credits for many weeks before a third Who 45, anthemic 'My Generation', ended 1965 one position short of unseating the Seekers' 'The Carnival Is Over' from the top.

Above: The Seekers
Below: The Who

February

PJ Proby's participation in a sold-out package tour on the ABC cinema circuit was curtailed when, after the expatriate Texan's tight velvet trousers split by accident during two previous shows, he was accused of contriving a repeat of the incident on a third occasion in Croydon. This was a godsend for then-hitless Welsh vocalist Tom Jones, who replaced Proby for the expedition's remaining dates. By March, Tom's latest single, 'It's Not Unusual', was at Number 1.

Initially, this was regrettable but not disastrous for Proby, who continued to climb the chart too with a reading of *West Side Story*'s 'Somewhere', delivered in a deep, swollen and affected baritone during a studio session that

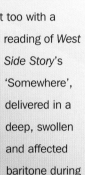

was, according to drummer Clem Cattini, 'hilarious. He sang lying on his back, completely blotto.' However, owing to the years of vocal extremity that have passed since, it didn't seem anywhere as ludicrous in 2006 when ol' PJ, more Falstaff than Flamineo now, sang it on a round-Britain swinging Sixties nostalgia presentation.

March

Lead guitarist Eric 'Slowhand' Clapton sensationally left the Yardbirds as they stood on the point of a Top 20 breakthrough with a third single, 'For Your Love'. Produced by bass player Paul Samwell-Smith, it featured an arresting tempo change and what a reviewer described as the 'sexy sound' of harpsichord and bongos. Fearing the London R&B group was 'selling out' with such a blatant bid for mainstream pop acceptance, Clapton would be readying himself for a tenure with John Mayall's Bluesbreakers, while his former colleagues – Samwell-Smith, drummer Jim

McCarty, singing mouth-organist Keith Relf and general factotum Chris Dreja – sought a replacement.

Though noted session player Jimmy Page resisted their overtures, he recommended Jeff Beck of the

Above: PJ Proby performing.
Middle: Welsh singer Tom Jones holding a single.
Below: The Yardbirds featuring Jeff Beck (second from right).

Tridents, an up-and-coming trio on the metropolitan club circuit. No Clapton duplicate, Beck's more adventurous solos and passagework displayed eclecticism and unpredictability in equal amounts. He was also game enough to clank around in a suit of armour during a crass promotional film short for 'For Your Love'.

The disc swept almost to the top at home and to Number 6 in the States. So began two years of back-to-back smashes – 'Heart Full Of Soul', 'Evil-Hearted You', 'Still I'm Sad', 'Shapes Of Things' and 'Over Under Sideways Down' – for one of the most groundbreaking outfits of the 1960s. Arguably, the earliest pop explorers of Indian music, they also investigated Gregorian chants and other eruditions, while remaining spellbinding on stage, chiefly through extended improvisations – or 'rave-ups' – as demonstrated on 1964's in-concert 'Five Live Yardbirds' and throughout a relentless international booking schedule that was among factors that led to the exits of Samwell-Smith and then Beck in 1966.

With Jimmy Page on board at last, an ailing Yardbirds struggled on as a four-piece until 1968 when they split in two: Relf and McCarty to form Renaissance eventually, and Page, following half-hearted rehearsals with a disinclined Dreja, to lead a New Yardbirds, who were to rack up heftier achievements when rechristened Led Zeppelin.

June

As epitomised by the *Daily Express*'s 'Long-Haired Monsters' headline, Britain's popular press felt duty-bound to inform readers that, after the Rolling Stones finished a UK tour at Romford ABC, Mick Jagger, Brian Jones and Bill Wyman, had urinated against a wall after being refused use of an East End petrol station's toilet. A private prosecution by Charles Keeley, the garage manager followed – for

doing so and not taking steps to 'conceal this act' – so he'd tell the bench when the case came up at West Ham Magistrates Court.

Fined for 'insulting behaviour', the Stones were also subjected to a judicial reprimand: 'Just because you have reached exalted heights in your profession, it does not mean that you can behave in this manner.' However, Dave Berry, another passenger in the car from which the three desperate men had spilled, would maintain, 'The pissing in the forecourt was blown out of proportion. A *Daily Mail* journalist was travelling with us, and it was his job to make the most of minor occurrences like that.'

Below: The Rolling Stones in 1965.

1960 1961 1962 1963 1964 **1965** 1966 1967 1968 1969

July

Outraged ticket-holders booed when Bob Dylan took the stage with a solid-body Stratocaster guitar at the Newport Folk Festival rather than his usual acoustic. He then compounded the upset by being accompanied by Chicago's all-electric Paul Butterfield Blues Band. Fans were already resentful that one side of his 'Bringing It All Back Home' LP, issued in May, had also been underpinned by amplified backing. Moreover, it embraced arrangements that reflected a captivation with British beat groups and their US imitators, who had reciprocated by covering Dylan items – as did the Animals with a retitled 'Baby Let Me Follow You Down' and, also from 1962's 'Bob Dylan' album, million-selling 'House Of The Rising Sun'. In 1964 too, Bob's 'If You Gotta Go, Go Now' had been a UK chart-topper for Manfred Mann, who he felt were the most effective interpreters of his work.

While Dylan was daring to 'go electric' at Newport, the Byrds were racing to the top on both sides of the Atlantic with their version of 'Bringing It All Back Home's 'Mr Tambourine Man'. This was a fusion of contemporary folk and Merseybeat via distinctively melodic four-part harmonies, and the uniquely spiralling effect of lead vocalist Jim (later, Roger) McGuinn's finger-picked twelve-string electric guitar. More insidiously, Dylan had influenced profoundly the disparate likes of 'Eve Of Destruction', Barry McGuire's all-purpose protest song, and 'I Got You Babe' by Sonny and Cher for those who found Dylan too harsh and impenetrable.

Though it meant sweating a bit over words, pop's more far-sighted composers were putting their minds to Dylan-type creations too. 'I'm A Loser', 'Shapes Of Things' and 1966's '19th Nervous Breakdown' by, respectively, the Beatles, the Yardbirds and the Rolling Stones, are three off-the-cuff examples that betrayed an absorption of Dylan, pre- and post-Newport, through constant replay of his albums.

1960 1961 1962 1963 1964 **1965** 1966 1967 1968 1969

Above: Bob Dylan in a pensive mood.
Below: *The Animals.*

SPORT

Stanley Matthews first professional footballer to be knighted

When Stanley Matthews retired from first-class football on 6 February 1965, he became the oldest player ever to appear in the First Division, then the game's top flight. Although he hadn't played for a year due to a knee injury, the teetotal vegetarian still set up the equaliser for his beloved Stoke City in his last match.

Born on 1 February 1915 in Stoke-on-Trent, Matthews became regarded as one of the greatest players England has ever produced. Nicknamed the Wizard of the Dribble, he left opposing defenders bewildered with his acceleration and bodyswerve.

Joining Stoke straight from school at the age of 14, he signed professional forms in 1932 and two years later made his international debut, scoring in England's 4-0 win over Wales. He would go on to score 11 times in 54 appearances for his country, the last in February 1957 making him the oldest player to pull on an England shirt.

Despite asking for a move in 1938 – a request that caused public outcry and protests in his home town – the intervention of the Second World War meant that he stayed on Stoke's books until his eventual £11,500 transfer to Blackpool in 1947.

It was at Bloomfield Road that Matthews enjoyed most success, notably in the 1953 FA Cup Final when his skills and awareness played an enormous part in Stan Mortensen's hat-trick and three years later he was voted the first ever European Footballer of the Year. He

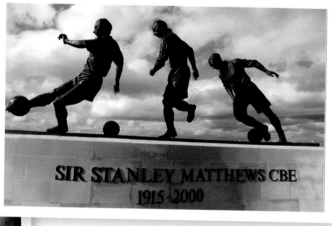

also collected the Football Writers' Player of the Year title in 1948 and 1963.

Rejoining Stoke City in 1961, he led them to the Second Division title two years later and, by the time he retired he had played 698 League games without ever being shown a yellow card.

He was carried off the field after his testimonial match in April 1965 shoulder-high by Lev Yashin (Russia) and Ferenc Puskas (Hungary) and, in the same year, became the first footballer to be knighted.

Sir Stanley died shortly after his eighty-fifth birthday in February 2000 and a statue has been erected at

Above and below: A tribute to Sir Stanley Matthews – his statue at the Britannia Stadium, Stoke City FC and aged 50, hanging up his boots for the last time.

Stoke's Britannia Stadium. In his honour, 1 February has been named Sir Stanley Matthews Day to raise money for his foundation that provides sports opportunities for local children.

Gary Player becomes only third man to win all four major championships

One of the best golfers the world has ever seen, Gary Player in 1965 joined Gene Sarazen (1935) and Ben Hogan (1953) as only the third man to win the four major titles of US Open, PGA Championship, the Open Championship – also known as the British Open – and the Masters. Jack Nicklaus (1966) and Tiger Woods (2000) have since equalled this feat.

Player was born in Johannesburg on 1 November 1935. One of the 'Big Three' with Arnold Palmer and Jack Nicklaus, he has registered more than 160 professional victories and lies equal fourth in the overall rankings with nine major championships behind Jack Nicklaus (18), Walter Hagen (11) and Tiger Woods (10).

Player, the son of a gold miner, turned professional in 1953 but was told two years later in England that he did not have what it took to become a successful golfer. In 1956, he won the first of his 13 South African Open titles and three years later became the youngest player to win the British Open!

Travelling more than 14 million miles during his career, Player is the only golfer in the twentieth century to have won the British Open in three different decades (1959, 1968 and 1974). One of his most amazing

comebacks came when he last won the Masters in 1978. Trailing the leaders by seven shots entering the final round, he registered birdies in seven out of the last ten holes to finish with a score of 64.

Known as the Black Knight, Player has been a successful competitor on the Senior Tour as well as designing more than 200 golf courses across the world and he also has a stud farm. He has been made an Honorary Doctor of Law by both St Andrews and Dundee University and an Honorary Doctor of Science by Northern Ireland's University of Ulster.

Above: Gary Player at the US Open golf tournament.

1960 1961 1962 1963 1964 1965 1966 1967 1968 1969

Freddie Mills found shot dead in Soho

Former World Light-Heavyweight boxing champion Freddie Mills (43) was found dead in a car in Soho, London, on 24 July 1965. A friend of the notorious Kray twins, he had been shot in the head, like so many associates of Ronnie and Reggie.

The official verdict was suicide but several theories have since been aired including that the nightclub owner and TV personality had been killed by Chinese gangsters or that Mills had

committed suicide after having been arrested and charged with homosexual indecency.

Mills, born in Parkstone on 26 June 1919, won the World Championship when he outfought American Gus Lesnevich over 15 rounds in July 1948. He lost the title on his first defence, being knocked out in the tenth round by another American, Joey Maxim, in January 1950. He retired after this defeat, finishing his career with a record of 75 wins (46 by knockout), 17 losses and five draws.

Above: The notorious Kray twins, Ronnie and Reggie.
Below: Hundreds attend the funeral procession of British Light-Heavyweight Champion Freddie Mills.

POLITICS & CURRENT AFFAIRS

Vietnam

There had been conflict in south-east Asia since the end of the Second World War in 1945, and by the early 1960s this conflict was focused on North and South Vietnam. The Communist North, led by Ho Chi Minh, was supported by the Soviet Union and China, while the democratic South was allied to Korea, Australia and the USA. Prior to 1965, the United States only had 'military advisers' in South Vietnam, but even so they sustained a significant number of casualties: In 1964, 136 Americans were killed and over 1,000 were wounded. Things could only get worse.

The conflict escalated in 1965, when in February the US launched air strikes on North Vietnam. Two months later, there were reports of napalm bombs being dropped on a Viet Cong stronghold in the South, near to the Cambodian border. Napalm was a defoliant, which 'turned the jungle into desert', and it was to be used on many subsequent occasions. In June 1965, United States forces were authorised by President Johnson to fight officially in a combat role, along with the South Vietnamese. Casualties mounted rapidly, and the innocent populations of nearby Laos and Cambodia became increasingly involved.

American involvement in Vietnam was to continue for many years, and the world became increasingly horrified by the whole affair. There had been opposition to the war in the United States from the beginning, but this intensified as the years went by. The Sixties was a decade of student protest and students across the globe, amongst many others, protested about Vietnam. In 1969 the US was forced to reduce the size of its force, and President Nixon finally withdrew it in 1973. It

Above: American napalm bombs exploding in fields south of Saigon during the Vietnam war.

was probably the best thing Nixon ever did, and the conflict finally ground to a halt in 1975. South Vietnam lost the war, but there were no winners.

Rhodesia declares UDI

During the early part of the decade, Britain tried to push Rhodesia into accepting black majority rule. Prime Minister Harold Wilson had been in discussion with Rhodesian leader Ian Smith on many occasions, but Smith simply wasn't having it. At times it seemed that some sort of compromise might be arrived at, but on 11 November 1965 Rhodesia produced its Universal Declaration of Independence (UDI) and challenged its former colonial masters to do something about it. The declaration was timed to coincide with Remembrance Day, with Smith pointing out the help and support

TO VOTE "YES" MEANS UNITY "NOT" U.D.I.

THE HON. I. D. SMITH. Prime Minister
PUBLISHED BY F. W. BRADBURN SECRETARY P.O. BOX 313, SALISBURY

Rhodesian troops had given to the mother country during World War Two.

The declaration came as a shock, but it was clear that the white Rhodesians meant business. Smith did however wish to remain loyal to the Crown, and he proposed that his newly independent country should retain the Queen as its sovereign. The Queen refused, and Britain imposed political and economic sanctions against the Smith regime. The United Nations joined in with the sanctions but they were not particularly effective, partly because there was

Above and below: A man crossing the street carrying a UDI election poster, in Salisbury, Rhodesia and how they were urged to vote 'Yes'.

as the Conservative member for Oldham. He later switched to the Liberal Party, before returning to the Conservative fold in 1924. While his political career was to have many ups and downs, he himself had seemed to be indestructible. Knighted in 1953, Churchill had stepped down as prime minister and Conservative Party leader in 1955, but remained an MP until 1964.

Sir Winston Churchill was awarded the rare honour of a state funeral. A total of 321,360 people filed past his coffin in Westminster Hall, in

a lot of 'sanction busting' and partly because the South African apartheid regime continued to trade openly with Rhodesia.

Although Ian Smith and his government wanted to maintain control by white Rhodesians for as long as possible, the new regime was not as oppressive as that of South Africa. There was some black representation under the new constitution, although many blacks who went along with it were regarded as puppets of the white regime. As the years went by, there was a gradual move towards the inevitable. In 1979 the country held its first truly multi-racial elections, and Britain again became briefly responsible for a state which was temporarily called Zimbabwe-Rhodesia. An independent Zimbabwe came into being in 1980.

Death of Churchill

Sir Winston Churchill died at the age of 90, following a stroke, on 24 January 1965. He was undoubtedly the most remarkable politician of the twentieth century, having been Britain's inspirational leader during World War Two. Churchill had first entered Parliament in 1900

the days before his funeral service at St. Paul's Cathedral. He was finally laid to rest at Bladon in Oxfordshire, close to his family home.

Above and below: Official portrait of Sir Winston Churchill taken to commemorate his 80th birthday just two months before his death, and his state funeral.

1966

FASHION, CULTURE & ENTERTAINMENT

Walt Disney dies

On 15 December 1966, Walt Disney died after a legendary career that transformed the entertainment industry. Born on 5 December 1901, Disney spent most of his childhood in Marceline, Missouri. He showed an early interest in art and often sold drawings to neighbours to make money. He studied art and photography and had a love of nature and wildlife. Despite a lack of funds, Walt's family encouraged his talents.

After a spell in France, driving an ambulance for the Red Cross – which he covered in cartoon characters – Walt returned to the US and pursued a career in

commercial art. After early bankruptcy with small company Laugh-O-Grams, he headed for Hollywood. *Alice Comedies* made him a leading Hollywood figure. He married and had two daughters.

Below and above right: Walt Disney with one of his greatest creations Mickey Mouse and holidaymakers enjoy Disneyland in California.

98

In 1932 *Flowers And Trees* won Walt the first of his Academy Awards and five years later he released *The Old Mill* which was the first short subject to use a camera technique called multi-plane. In that same year, *Snow White And The Seven Dwarf*s became the first full-length animated musical feature to be released. Over the following five years, Walt Disney Studios released other classic animations including, *Dumbo*, *Pinocchio*, *Bambi* and *Fantasia*.

Disneyland opened in 1955, realising Walt's dream of a clean, organised amusement park. One year earlier, as a television pioneer, he also began production for the small screen and was innovative in full-colour programming. To many, Walt Disney is a legend whose worldwide popularity, and that of his films, is still as high today as it was during his heyday.

Mary Quant and the miniskirt

Like John Bates, who designed the plastic dress and outfits for Diana Rigg in *The Avengers*, Mary Quant was an innovative designer who quickly established that the youth of the 1960s had money and wanted to spend it

on fashion. Not the sensible two-piece outfits and comfortable cardigans their parents wore, but stylish designs that made a statement.

Mary Quant began her career as an amateur having studied illustration at Goldsmith's College and having had a job with a couture milliner. She came to the conclusion that fashion should be accessible to everyone, youth included. Her insight was coupled with her ability to cater for the 1960s fashion scene despite having no formal business training.

Quant opened her own design house and in 1955 she opened one of her first boutiques, Bazaar on the Kings Road. Unsatisfied with the range of clothes she was able to find for the boutique, and having been designing and making her own clothes, Quant decided that she would have to make clothes for the boutique

1960 1961 1962 1963 1964 1965 **1966** 1967 1968 1969

Above: Mary Quant, in a trademark white dress with black collar, shows off the OBE she had just received from the Queen.

herself. She was responsible for many introductions to the Mod era and she invented the Chelsea Look.

There were many designers who claimed to have created the miniskirt but it is widely accepted that Mary Quant, if not the first to design the skirt, was certainly at the forefront of its rise and popularity. Quant was certainly responsible for replacing stockings and suspenders with tights, which made the miniskirt easier to wear. Some of her best-selling clothing included small white collars attached to a black jumper or dress and black stretch tights.

By 1963, she was exporting to the US and launched the Ginger Group in order to keep up with demand. Mary Quant was presented with the *Sunday Times* International Award for shaking the UK out of its conventional attitude to clothes. As her reputation grew,

she created the micro-mini and 'paint box' make up of 1966 and she launched her own range of cosmetics. She received the OBE for her contribution to the fashion industry.

Spaghetti Westerns: *The Good, The Bad and The Ugly*

Between 1961 and 1975, European film-makers made around 600 Westerns, which European audiences loved. Critics were less enthusiastic about the films and they were dubbed Spaghetti Westerns due to the fact that most were backed by Italian companies.

In 1961, Michael Carreras' Spanish-produced *Savage Guns*, starring Richard Basehart, proved that a well-produced Western could be made on foreign soil. The

Below and above: Clint Eastwood the 'Man with no name' and in showdown action.

Again starring Clint Eastwood and Lee Van Cleef with Eli Wallach, this Civil War epic is considered the quintessential Spaghetti Western. With music from Ennio Morricone and widescreen cinematography from Tonino Delli Colli, the film remains the most prolific of all Spaghetti Westerns.

Action Man

In 1966, Palitoy, a UK subsidiary of General Mills, launched a new boy's action figure, Action Man into the toy market. Although modelled on the American GI Joe, the figure reflected a British military theme and had a range of equipment and accessories, although American outfits and equipment were also produced.

One of Palitoy's innovations was flocked hair and the first Action Man figures included Action Soldier, Action Sailor and Action Pilot in outfits from World War Two. Over the years, outfits and equipments kept up the military theme and British units and equipment were

only really good Westerns up to this point were all filmed and produced in the US. Sergio Leone, a little-known director at the time, enjoyed huge success with *A Fistful Of Dollars* and producers began financing more and more films of the genre.

In 1965, Leone directed the sequel *For A Few Dollars More*, teaming Clint Eastwood and retired actor Lee Van Cleef as rival bounty hunters. This second film secured Leone's reputation as a director of Westerns and, in 1966, he directed the last in the trilogy with *The Good, The Bad And The Ugly*.

1960 1961 1962 1963 1964 1965 **1966** 1967 1968 1969

Below: A young boy examines a display of Action Man toys at the British Toy Fair in Brighton.

produced. There were also non-military action figures who covered other activities such as mountain rescue, arctic exploration and deep sea diving.

Larger accessories proved popular including the Scorpion tank, the Ferret armoured car and the Land Rover. Today, although the figure is still popular, there is no military theme and Action Man is sold as a modern adventurer.

Go-Go Boots

Also known as kinky boots, go-go boots became a fashion fetish when actress Honor Blackman wore a pair for her role as Cathy Gale in the hit television series, *The Avengers*. And, in January 1966, when Nancy Sinatra topped the Top 40 charts with 'These Boots Are Made For Walking', the boots had risen from ankle-height to knee-high. In her white go-go boots, Sinatra was virtually every man's fantasy and soon young women everywhere were wearing them.

Designed by André Courrèges in the early 1960s, go-go boots were shiny white, PVC, low-heeled boots that came slightly above the ankle. They were boots popular with teen dancers who found them much more comfortable than the spike-heeled dress shoes of the time. The boots were quickly named go-go boots after the go-go dancers who wore them. Prior to that, for most of the twentieth century, boots had only been worn as essential footwear for working, riding or bad weather.

MUSIC

February

RCA's fastest-selling disc of 1966 was 'The Ballad Of The Green Berets' by Staff Sergeant Barry Sadler. Without naming names, it lent uncompromising support to the US presence in Vietnam, and made hearts swell with patriotic pride when, standing smartly to attention in full battledress, Sadler even piped it out on TV pop showcase *American Bandstand*.

A ruggedly handsome veteran not yet thirty, his picture had adorned chin-up publications recounting the deeds of the lads in the front line. One of these was *The Green Berets* by Robin Moore, who submitted lyrics to Sadler, an amateur songwriter. Together, they came up with the jingoistic, slow-march ballad that, within a fortnight of release, was a US Number 1.

Below: Nancy Sinatra wearing her white go-go boots.

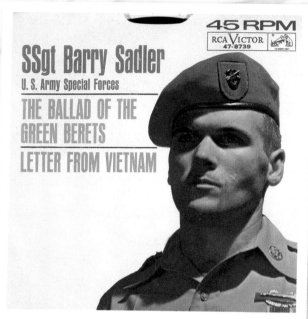

Next, a Private Charles Bowen was found to record 'Christmas In Vietnam', which just missed a December sell-in already clogged with the likes of Ric King's 'Hymn To A Returning Soldier' and 'An Open Letter To My Teenage Son' from Victor Lundberg as one still over there. None sold particularly well, but there were a lot of them.

March

John Lennon's ruminations about religion in London's *Evening Standard* were reprinted out of context in *Datebook*, a US teenage periodical. Weightier journals sensationalised further an implication that the arch-Beatle had 'boasted' that his group were more popular than Christ – though, if anything, John, in the original article, had seemed to be bemoaning the increasing godlessness of the times.

It was, however, interpreted as 'blasphemy' by enough US readers to worry Brian Epstein into trying to cancel the North American leg of what turned out to be the Beatles' final tour. There were real fears of an assassination attempt on Lennon, particularly in the Deep South where thousands of Beatles records were being ceremonially pulverised in a tree-grinding machine to the running commentary of a local media personality. 'Revolver', the group's new album, was removed from 22 southern radio playlists and a proposed Beatles session in Sun Studios, where Elvis Presley's recording career had begun, was subsequently cancelled.

At a press conference hours before opening night in Chicago on 12 August, Lennon was trotted out to make a statement that most took as an apology – and engagements in northern stadiums passed without incident. Below the Mason-Dixon line, 'I Love John' lapel badges outsold all associated merchandise.

Above: Staff Sergeant Barry Sadler on the sleeve of the record of 'The Ballad of the Green Berets'.
Below: The Beatles pose in a window at Twickenham Film Studios.

1969 1968 1967 1966 1965 1964 1963 1962 1961 1960

Nevertheless, a firework that exploded on the boards in Memphis was unnerving in the light of a telephoned death threat that afternoon. Elsewhere, there were picketings outside auditoriums by Ku Klux Klansmen and attempted peltings of the Fab Four with decayed fruit and more odious projectiles.

Never had arguments against continued stage appearances made more sense, and so it was that the Beatles downed tools as a working band at San Francisco's Candlestick Park on 29 August 1966.

April

While it forgot to print the group's name, a gushing *New Musical Express* review of 'Wild Thing' by the Troggs coincided with a sprinkling of spins on pirate radio to set in motion its rapid rise to the edge of the Top 10. With this news, lead singer Reg Presley resigned immediately from his day job as an Andover bricklayer, rounded up the other Troggs – guitarist Chris Britton, drummer Ronnie Bond and, on bass, Pete Staples – and drove post-haste to manager Larry Page's office in London to try to resolve what was a good problem to have.

Garbed in a new stage uniform, the lads plugged the disc on ITV's *Thank Your Lucky Stars* the following Saturday. This set in motion a clamber to a high of Number 2 – with only 'Paint It Black' by the Rolling

Stones preventing the Troggs from lording it on *Top Of The Pops*. After similar performances in European and Australasian charts, it scrambled to pole position in the US Hot 100, and 'Troggs On Top Of The World' blazed from the front page of the *Andover Advertiser*.

The three-chord directness of the Troggs triggered bemused comment about the depths to which pop had sunk, and was to pigeonhole them for all time as the Unthinking Man's Pop Group. 'They're so far behind, they're in front,' sniggered Graham Nash of The Hollies.

This was all grist to the publicity mill, especially as the Troggs were being projected as rustic ingenues.

Above: The Troggs attempting to leave a lift, all at the same time!

They tried to remain polite when folk made unkind remarks about them, biting back on even admissible expletives like cr*p and bl**dy. A few years later, however, an enterprising engineer was to record one of the group's studio discussions and bootlegged it as 'The Troggs Tape' – though it was to be issued officially on vinyl in 1980 as a joy forever for a wider public.

May

Brian Wilson's decision to concentrate on composition and production back in California while his fellow Beach Boys continued a hectic touring schedule with a replacement was vindicated with the release of his – and the group's – greatest album. If ever Brian's clever stuff with its tempo changes and counterpoint proved weak commercially, the balance could be redressed with a revival of, say, the Regents' 'Barbara Ann' or old folk songs like 'Sloop John B', the only non-original on *Pet Sounds*, the most critically acclaimed album the Beach Boys ever released.

Creating a recurring mood – a 'concept' if you like – it was inspirational to the Beatles as they prepared *Sgt Pepper's Lonely Hearts Club Band* – with Paul McCartney citing Wilson as 'the real contender' rather than the Rolling Stones. Yet *Pet Sounds* was only a moderate seller at the time – though its spin-off singles, 'Sloop John B' and 'God Only Knows', were both big hits.

1960 1961 1962 1963 1964 1965 **1966** 1967 1968 1969

Below: The Beach Boys.

1960 1961 1962 1963 1964 1965 1966 1967 1968 1969

October

Britain's foremost 'underground' newspaper, *International Times (IT)*, was sped on its way with a 'happening' on a cold night in London's barn-like Roundhouse auditorium where proto-flower children milled around with celebrities like Michelangelo 'Blow Up' Antonioni – the artiest mainstream film director of the mid-1960s – and Marianne Faithfull in a cross between a nun's habit and buttock-revealing miniskirt. Thousands more than can have actually been there reminisce now about the free sugar-cubes that may or may not have contained LSD, and the ectoplasmic light-shows that were part of the feedback-ridden act for the Pink Floyd and the Soft Machine (in days before the definite article was removed from their names).

In its 1967 to 1969 prime, *IT* leaked to back-street newsagents as the provincial hipster's vista to what swinging London was thinking and doing. Sporadic

Above: *Members of the rock group Soft Machine.*
Below: *The Roundhouse auditorium.*

editions were still appearing in the next decade, but *IT* petered out soon after joining forces with *Oz* – regarded spuriously as its 'colour supplement' – to produce *FREEk*, a daily broadsheet for an Isle of Wight pop festival.

SPORT

England World Cup

England's football team had qualified for four previous tournaments under Walter Winterbottom but despite their stature in the global game they had yet to make any mark in the World Cup.

With the arrival of Alf Ramsey as manager following the team's quarter-final exit at the hands of eventual winners Brazil in 1962, England had time to prepare for the tournament they were hosting.

Their first game in Group 1 turned out to be a disappointing 0-0 draw with Uruguay but they bounced back to overcome a resilient Mexico in the following match. Manchester United's Bobby Charlton scored a trademark blockbuster just before half-time and Roger Hunt (Liverpool) added a second. France were the opponents for the third game and were disposed of thanks to two Hunt goals.

Much had been expected of Spurs striker Jimmy Greaves in the pre-tournament build-up, but he sustained an injury and was replaced by West Ham's

Below: Bobby Charlton volleys the ball during the World Cup Final at Wembley Stadium.

1960 1961 1962 1963 1964 1965 1966 1967 1968 1969

Geoff Hurst for the quarter-final against Argentina and it was he who scored the only goal of an ill-tempered game. Portugal were waiting in the semi-final and, despite Eusebio netting from the penalty spot, two goals from Bobby Charlton booked England's place in the Final against West Germany.

Helmut Haller drew first blood after 13 minutes but Hurst equalised just six minutes later and that was how it remained for another hour. Hurst's West Ham team-mate Martin Peters slotted home a rebound to send the home supporters wild but the Germans scored a last-gasp equaliser through Wolfgang Weber to send the game into extra-time.

A second goal from Hurst gave England the advantage and sparked furious protests from the Germans who claimed the ball never crossed the line after hitting the crossbar. As fans started to flood the pitch thinking the referee had blown the final whistle, Hurst completed his hat-trick to give the hosts a 4-2 win.

All their matches had been played at Wembley and England became only the third hosts to win the tournament after Uruguay (1930) and Italy (1934).

British Commonwealth Games held in Kingston, Jamaica

It was Reverend Astley Cooper who in 1891 proposed that the British Empire Games be held every four years with its aim of increasing the goodwill and understanding of the British Empire.

Above: Bobby Moore proudly holds the 'Jules Rimet' World Cup trophy after England defeated West Germany in the final.

REMEMBER THE SIXTIES

The Festival of the Empire was staged in 1911 in London as part of the celebrations surrounding the coronation of King George V. The Inter-Empire Championships which saw teams from Australia, Canada and South Africa competing with the Home Nations, was an integral part. But it was not until 1928 that Canadian Melville Marks Robinson was asked to organise the first event and this was held in Ontario two years later.

Now known as the British Commonwealth Games, the 1966 event, held in Kingston, Jamaica, was notable for being the first to be hosted by a non-white Commonwealth country. The Home Nations – England, Scotland, Wales and Northern Ireland – as always sent separate teams and were joined by many

fencing, swimming and diving, weightlifting and wrestling made up the other disciplines.

England topped the medal table with 33 golds, including all eight in the men's and women's fencing events. Australia came second in the table and claimed ten out of the 13 gold medals on offer in the men's swimming.

England's Mary Rand and Wales' Lynn Davies both scored gold in the long jump to go with the Olympic titles they had won two years earlier. Scotland (Jim Alder in the Marathon), Northern Ireland (James McCourt in the light-welterweight boxing) and the Isle of Man (Peter Buckley in the road race) all finished with one gold medal apiece.

British overseas territories, with many such as Antigua and Mauritius competing for the first time.

The event programme was altered for the first time since 1950 with lawn bowls and rowing being replaced with badminton and shooting. Athletics, boxing, cycling,

1960 1961 1962 1963 1964 1965 **1966** 1967 1968 1969

Above: Long jumper Lynn Davies.
Below: Ron Wallwork of England raises his arms in victory as he reaches the finish line of the 30 kilometres road walk at the Commonwealth Games.

Wales win a third consecutive Five Nations

The mid-1960s belonged to the Wales Rugby Union team as they won three consecutive Five Nations titles between 1964-66. With the demise of coal mining and steel production in the Principality, it was the turn of school-teachers and doctors to don the red jersey with pride.

The 1964 title had to be shared with Scotland following draws with England and France while a Triple Crown was secured the following year (a 22-13 reverse in Paris the only downside to a successful campaign).

Wales kicked off the 1966 season with an 11-6 win over England at Twickenham, captain Alun Pask – a Five Nations regular over the three seasons – scoring the visitors' only try of the game. Home victories over Scotland (8-3, including two tries from centre Ken Jones) and France (9-8) sandwiched a 9-6 defeat at Landsdowne Road as Ireland prevented Wales from retaining their Triple Crown and adding the Grand Slam.

Above: *Wales take on France at Cardiff Arms Park.*

POLITICS & CURRENT AFFAIRS

Labour increase majority

After a couple of years in power, and working with a very small majority, Prime Minister Harold Wilson believed that the Labour Party was now popular enough to win a majority of a more substantial nature. Having enhanced his 'man of the people' image by constantly smoking a pipe, wearing Gannex raincoats, pretending to have HP Sauce with everything, going on holiday to the Scilly Isles and ensuring that the Beatles each got an MBE, he decided it was now time to capitalise, and to go to the country once more.

Accordingly, on 31 March 1966, the people of Britain went to the polls. The methods employed by pollsters to gauge the likely results of elections were less sophisticated then and, although another Labour victory was widely predicted, the outcome was not all that certain. The Conservative Party was however still going though a bad patch, and Wilson's policies had generally gone down rather well at the beginning of the swinging Sixties. In addition, a

1960 1961 1962 1963 1964 1965 1966 1967 1968 1969

Above and below: Harold Wilson, as often portrayed, smoking a pipe and newly re-elected members of the Labour Government on the front bench.

recent by-election in Hull had suggested that Labour was on something of a roll.

In the event, Labour did win a substantial majority in the new parliament. A total of 363 seats went their way (an increase of 48 over the 1964 election) while the Tories won 242 and the Liberals just 12. Wilson had an overall majority of 96. He stood outside Number 10, beaming broadly and puffing on his pipe although, in private, he much preferred to smoke cigars. He was to enjoy another four years as Prime Minister, before being temporarily ousted by Edward Heath. This setback did not cause him to lose the leadership of his party however, and Harold Wilson was later to bounce back to win two further elections in 1974.

Cultural revolution

Mao Tse-Tung had led China since the communist revolution of 1949. He was a ruthless dictator who had caused the deaths of millions, but he had at least pleased many millions of peasants by declaring that they now owned the land upon which they worked. During the 1950s, improvements in agricultural production seemed to cement his power base. However, by 1966, growing unrest in the country led to the creation of what became known as the Cultural Revolution. Chairman Mao, probably fearing that his dictatorship was at risk if he didn't do something radical, encouraged students and workers to rise up against the party bureaucrats and take power from them.

The so-called Red Guards were duly formed, and revolutionary committees were set up to take over from the old guard of the Communist Party. It was, needless to say, total chaos. In the interest of 'purifying the party', intellectuals and people considered to be guilty of bourgeois thought, were persecuted and arrested. Intellectual pursuits were largely banned and millions were forced to do manual labour. Thousands of innocent people – many of them dedicated communists – were executed. If China's economic structure was

Above and below: A group of Chinese children in uniform holding Mao's 'Little Red Book' during China's Cultural Revolution and Mao Tse Tung, President of Red China.

dodgy to begin with, it fell into complete ruin during Mao's new revolution.

The worst of the mayhem and chaos lasted until 1969, although things did not get much better until Mao's death in 1976. It was then decided, by those that had not actually starved to death or been killed during the preceding ten years, that the Cultural Revolution had not perhaps been such a good idea after all. It was time to move on, after a fashion, and a group known as the Gang of Four were blamed for the whole depressing and evil business. One of these was Chairman Mao's widow, Jiang Qing.

The Aberfan disaster

At 9.15 a.m. on 21 October 1966, a coal waste tip began to slide down a mountainside in South Wales.

The slide quickly gathered momentum, and within minutes the coal waste had smothered and killed 144 people, including 116 children, in the mining village of Aberfan. Pantglas Junior School was engulfed, and inside more than half its pupils, as well as five teachers, were to die. Twenty small houses were also destroyed, and again many people were killed. It took almost a week to recover all the bodies.

News of the disaster quickly spread around the world, and a disaster fund eventually raised more than £1.6 million for the families of the victims. Welsh mining villages had always had their share of disasters, but none was as great as this. The inevitable Inquiry blamed the National Coal Board for the disaster, as safety standards had not been observed, but this was of little comfort to the people of Aberfan.

Below: The scene in Aberfan after part of the village school was engulfed by a giant coal slag heap.

1960 1961 1962 1963 1964 1965 **1966** 1967 1968 1969

1960 1961 1962 1963 1964 1965 1966 1967 1968 1969

1967

FASHION, CULTURE & ENTERTAINMENT

Radio 1 is born

At the request of the then government in response to pirate radio stations such as Radio Caroline – a European radio station transmitting offshore on a boat anchored in international waters somewhere off the south-east coast – Radio 1 was launched at 7.00 a.m. on 30 September 1967.

Below: Ex-pirate disc jockeys, lining up to join the BBC. (left to right) Pete Drummond, Mike Raven, Tony Blackburn, Dave Cash, Chris Denning, Duncan Johnson (behind), Ed Stewart, Mike Ahern, John Peel, Emperor Rosko, Mike Lennox and kneeling Kenny Everett.

With Radio 1 being aimed at the 16-24 year-old aged group, Radio 1's first DJ was Tony Blackburn who chose to play 'Flowers In The Rain' by the Move with his cheery '…and, good morning everyone. Welcome to the exciting new sound of Radio 1'. The station became hugely popular with a pop music format by day and rock/progressive music by night.

Initially broadcast on 1214 kHz medium wave, in 1978 it moved to 1053/1089 kHz and was allowed to take over Radio 2's FM transmitters for a few hours a week – most notably on a Sunday afternoon for the Top 40 singles chart. In 1988, Radio 1 was granted its own FM network. Under BBC licensing laws, Radio 1, like other BBC stations, is unable to broadcast commercials and is financed through a licence fee.

Changes in the mid-1990s by controller Matthew Bannister were fortuitous. The station's DJs and listeners were all aging and he sought to make the station for the under-25s once again, bringing in younger DJs. Britpop was on the rise and bands like Oasis, Blur and Pulp helped the station's popularity rise once more. Many of the DJs ousted from Radio 1 by Bannister moved to Radio 2, which has overtaken Radio 1 as the UK's most popular radio station, with a style that Radio 1 had up until the early 1990s. Annie Nightingale is today the station's longest-serving presenter, having joined Radio 1 in 1969.

The Beatles broadcast to 400 million

On 25 June 1967, the Beatles became the first band ever to be globally transmitted on television to an estimated 400 million people worldwide. The reason: *Our World* was the first live international satellite television production with performers from 26 countries, all invited to take part in the six-hour event, in order to spread a message of peace to the world.

The Beatles represented the UK and John Lennon wrote 'All You Need Is Love' especially for the broadcast which was recorded in black and white. Friends Mick Jagger, Eric Clapton, Marianne Faithfull, Keith Moon and Graham Nash among others all showed up and sang along with the band for the performance which was done after one take in rehearsal.

Having been asked to contribute a song with a simple message that would be understood by the audience of different nationalities, Lennon's song extended the

1960 1961 1962 1963 1964 1965 1966 **1967** 1968 1969

Above: The Move whose record 'Flowers In The Rain' was the first to be played on Radio 1.
Below: The Beatles prepare for 'Our World'.

message he had tried to put across in 'The Word'. The song was inspired, the message simple and it is impossible to misinterpret what Lennon was saying in the song. He was to describe the song later as propaganda. The band decided 'All You Need Is Love' should be their next single and it was released on 7 July 1967, went straight to Number 1 and remained there for three weeks.

For the 'Our World' live performance the song was given an international feel and included the French national anthem, snatches of JS Bach, 'Greensleeves' and 'In The Mood' by Glenn Miller.

Barbarella

The film *Barbarella*, released in 1967, was based on a French adult comic strip which began life in 1962, and starred a young Jane Fonda in the leading role. Fonda had turned down leading roles in *Rosemary's Baby* and *Bonnie And Clyde* having been shown the script for *Barbarella* by Italian producer Dino De Laurentiis (who

Above: The Beatles at a rehearsal for their global TV performance with an expected audience of 400 million.

plastic and PVC as well as see-through clothing, cat-suits and thigh-length boots. Costumes were designed by Jaques Fonteray who ensured that *Barbarella* was the most fashion-conscious space fantasy at the time.

Based on Jean-Claude Forest's original film of the comic strip, Barbarella is called to see the President of Earth as she is the only five star double-rated astronavigatrix who can save the universe. Her nemesis is scientist Duran Duran, who is hiding a weapon (the Positronic Ray) designed to destroy the loving union of the universe that has been enjoyed for centuries.

later made *Flash Gordon)*. Filming started at De Laurentiis's studios in Rome with Fonda's then husband, Roger Vadim, as director.

Set in the fortieth century, *Barbarella* is an erotic romp through space with Vadim's view of space depicted in a fantasy world of sensual, tactile surfaces, plastics and fur while Fonda immortalised the space-cadet look with back-combed hair, false eyelashes and bizarre, minimalist outfits in

1960 1961 1962 1963 1964 1965 1966 **1967** 1968 1969

Below: Promotional poster for the film, 'Barbarella', directed by Roger Vadim and starring Jane Fonda.

The Monkees

The Monkees released their first Number 1 hit in the UK with 'I'm A Believer' in 1967. They were the first manufactured boy-band, formed in 1965 in LA, California, and were also the stars of a US television series of the same name aired on NBC from 1966-68.

At their peak, they were one of the most popular musical acts of their time, eventually disbanding in 1970. After several reunions, the Monkees last worked together in 2001.

The band members were Davy Jones on percussion, vocals and guitar, Micky Dolenz Jr (drums, guitar, vocals), Mike Nesmith (guitar, vocals, keyboard), and Peter 'Tork' Thorkelson (bass, keyboards, vocals).

The show featured the antics of a fictional pop-rock group which due to the massive success of their records and public expectation became a real pop group. The success of the first season of the show saw the four

Above: The Monkees performing onstage in an episode of their self-titled TV show.

Below: A 40ft psychedelic mural on the wall of the Beatles' 'Apple' boutique.

members of the band featured on January's *TV Guide* in 1967. The four members had been chosen from 437 hopefuls. The Monkees won two Emmy Awards in 1967 for Outstanding Comedy Series and Outstanding Directorial Achievement in Comedy.

Summer of love, flower power and paisley designs

The hippie culture was born when reaction to the war in Vietnam caused students and young people to give up on society and form their own counter-culture. Flower power became a widespread term as many hippies felt they got their 'power' from the cannabis flower and flowery clothing became popular.

Hippie fashion reached its peak in 1967 with psychedelic 'alternative' outfits such as kaftans, afghan coats, body paint and flowers worn in their hair. The most popular types of clothes were tie-dyes, bellbottom trousers, patched blue jeans, love beads, flowery patterned bandanas, long dresses, Nehru jackets, paisley fabrics and velvet.

The summer of 1967 is known as the Summer of Love when the hippie movement came to full fruition, particularly in the district of Haight-Ashbury in San Francisco. The Summer of Love began with a prelude at the Human Be-In which took place in San Francisco's Golden Gate Park on 14 January that same year and introduced the word psychedelic to the masses. It was a celebration of hippie culture and values.

MUSIC

February

37-year-old Joe Meek, tormented by financial and mental disintegration, chose the eighth anniversary of Buddy Holly's death to squeeze a fatal twelve-bore trigger on both his complaining landlady and himself in his cramped RGM Sound studio in north London, littered with what looked to Geoff Goddard, the studio's most renowned in-house songwriter, 'like odds and ends he'd picked up from a junk shop, wired it all up and made something of it. He didn't have the capital for much else.'

Yet, if he became as tragic a pop legend as Holly, many of Meek's innovations as an independent console boffin changed recording procedures forever, and his inventive cauldron of other-worldliness, funfair vulgarity and catchy tunes are synonymous with the early 1960s while simultaneously prime examples of recording art.

1960 1961 1962 1963 1964 1965 1966 **1967** 1968 1969

Below: Joe Meek at work in his bedroom studio in Holloway Road, London.

REMEMBER THE SIXTIES

Wraithful 'Johnny Remember Me' from 1961 – with film actor John Leyton on lead vocals – almost returned to Number 1 a quarter of a century later as part of 'I Feel Love', a medley by Bronski Beat and Marc Almond. Moreover, under Meek's aegis too, the Tornados realised the timeless 'Telstar', and surfaced as the only serious challengers to the Shadows as the foremost British instrumental unit. If unable to build on a chartbuster in North America with 'Telstar', the outfit scored three more entries – 'Globetrotter', 'Robot' and 'The Ice Cream Man' – in 1963's domestic Top 20 before the levelling blow of Merseybeat with its emphasis on vocals.

Tetchy, opinionated and paranoid, Meek's splendid certainty about everything he said and did seemed justified too in summer 1964 when his 'Have I The Right' by the Honeycombs topped the charts, though it was the most fruitful of many expedient concessions to the group boom – which Meek regarded as a passing fad – as storm clouds gathered. Nonetheless, Geoff Goddard observed that 'at times, even then, he would relax, but he was like Jekyll and Hyde. Basically, Joe wasn't a businessman. Every record was a struggle.'

Mistaking Brian Jones for fellow Rolling Stone Mick Jagger, two *News Of The World* witch-hunters had cobbled together a report assuring readers, several months after the fact, that he had invited them back to his flat to smoke some hashish – or was it LSD? When an enraged Jagger served a libel suit, the editor carpeted the hacks responsible and plotted a damage-

Below: The Honeycombs.

This defence was to be overruled at West Sussex Quarter Sessions in June, and so was Richards' remarkably cool and articulate account of himself in the dock. The jury returned a guilty verdict on both Stones who were jailed – Mick for three months, Keith for a year – amid extravagant rejoicing and lamentation in the media. After not quite two days behind bars, the two were granted bail when awaiting an ultimately successful appeal.

The best-known drugs trial in pop 'gave the Stones this image of being like a real bunch of dope fiends,' shrugged Jagger, chief advocate of the rush-released 'We Love You', the Stones' mock-conciliatory riposte to an ugly situation. Bracketed by prison-door sound

limitation scheme whereby the truth – or *a* truth – could be re-timed. By prodding various nerves, he discovered that Jagger and girlfriend Marianne Faithfull were to spend a weekend at Redlands, Keith Richards' moated grange near Chichester. It was a matter of a couple of telephone calls to the local police station to arrange for the place to be invaded on the Sunday evening.

Sure enough, the officers found enough 'substances' to warrant the arrest of Richards and – to the *News Of The World*'s relief – Jagger, even if his charge had to be trumped up from four pep pills that were available over the counter *sur le continent*, and that his doctor had permitted him to retain to combat pressure of work.

Above: Mick Jagger and Keith Richards leaving the Appeals court in London, after they had been charged for illegal possession of drugs.
Below: Singer Marianne Faithfull.

1960 1961 1962 1963 1964 1965 1966 **1967** 1968 1969

REMEMBER THE SIXTIES

effects, it was, with Procol Harum's 'A Whiter Shade Of Pale' and 'All You Need Is Love' by the Beatles, the summer's most plugged 45 on the playlist of pirate Radio London, then awaiting its final hour when the Marine Offences Act became law in August.

In the UK Top 10, the sweetcorn peddled by Engelbert Humperdinck and Tom Jones sat awkwardly amid the psychedelics of the Move, the Jimi Hendrix Experience and the Pink Floyd, demonstrating that the opposite of a prevailing trend is always represented in the charts to some degree – but what was the prevailing trend? 1967, see, was a boom time for schmaltz with Humperdinck's 'Release Me' keeping the Beatles' latest from the top later that month, and his 'The Last Waltz' serving Traffic the same in autumn.

Petula Clark, Harry Secombe, Des O'Connor and even post-war balladeer Donald Peers groped into the Top 20 too. Tellingly, after all his R&B records had failed, Long John Baldry joined this syrupy elite with 'Let The Heartaches Begin' during a counter-revolution tacitly applauded by commentators like the *New Musical Express*'s 'Alley Cat' tittle-tattler, who fawned over elderly

record business executives – 'Pye chief Louis Benjamin predicts Number 1 for Long John Baldry' – whilst gloating, 'This year, Yardbirds absent from Top 30'.

June

San Francisco had become as vital a pop Mecca as Liverpool had been when the Monterey International

Below: Jimi Hendrix holds an award which he has just received from Radio One DJ Jimmy Savile.
Middle: Members of Pink Floyd.

Yet Jimi's name would be dropped in 'Monterey', a piece of musical journalism soon to be a US hit by another act on the bill, Eric Burdon and his New Animals. Like Burdon and Hendrix, Brian Jones – with Nico of the Velvet Underground – was noticed ambling around the site, attracting none of the clothes-tearing commotion that there might have been anywhere innocent of Californian *sang-froid*.

December

Georgia soul shouter Otis Redding and all but one of his Stax record label's second-string resident band, the Bar-Kays, plus his valet and the crew perished after their wind-buffeted aircraft dived into icy Lake Monoma near Madison, Wisconsin. The previous week, 26-year-old Otis had recorded a new single, '(Sittin' On) The Dock Of The Bay'. Its self-penned lyrics were flavoured with a soupçon of premonition, but its ascent to the top at home, Number 3 in Britain, was not totally on 'sympathy' sales, far from it, as it was also Redding's most direct attempt on disc to become the darling of more than just soul connoisseurs. Towards this end, he'd also had the self-confidence to revive '(I Can't Get No) Satisfaction' as a Top 40 hit within weeks of it being the first of many Rolling Stones US Number 1s. Thrown together on a long-haul flight that same year, Otis and Roy Orbison had mulled over the feasibility of making an album together, even bestowing it with a provisional title, 'Big O: Black And White Soul'.

Pop Festival was held a few miles down the coast. It was here that the Who capitalised on their first unarguable US smash, 'Happy Jack' – and Jimi Hendrix's showmanship as much as his fretboard dexterity spurred a gallop to international stardom. Among further highlights was an afternoon set by Indian sitar master Ravi Shankar, who'd been appalled by Hendrix 'when he started being obscene with his guitar and burning it. I come from a different part of the world where we respect, almost worship the instruments.'

1960 1961 1962 1963 1964 1965 1966 **1967** 1968 1969

Above: Otis Redding.

1969 1968 1967 1966 1965 1964 1963 1962 1961 1960

SPORT

Donald Campbell dies

Donald Campbell – the son of Sir Malcolm Campbell who broke the world land speed record nine times between 1924-35 in a succession of cars named *Bluebird* – continued the family's record-breaking tradition after his father's 1949 death after a long illness.

Donald, born on 23 March 1921, initially concentrated on the water speed record, but he struggled with the *K4* boat his father used and suffered a 170mph crash in 1951. The development of a new *K7* boat saw him set seven world water speed records between 1955-64, the first at Ullswater where he hit 202mph culminating in a speed of 276.33mph at Lake Dumbleyung in Australia.

Donald then began to attack the land speed record and succeeded in setting a new world record of 403.1mph at Australia's Lake Eye so becoming the first person to simultaneously hold the world record on both land and water.

Then on 4 January 1967 on Coniston Water he crashed and died while attempting to become the first person to go over 300mph on water. Achieving a remarkable 297mph in the jet-powered *Bluebird* on the first run, he turned around without refuelling but – more crucially – he did not wait for his wake to settle before setting off on the return.

At a speed of more than 300mph, *Bluebird's* nose lifted out of the water and the boat somersaulted and disintegrated on landing on the surface. He was heard to say on the radio 'She's going – she's going. I'm almost on my back.' His helmet, shoes, oxygen mask and mascot were recovered but there was no trace of his body.

On 8 March 2001, against the wishes of most locals, *Bluebird* was recovered from Coniston Water where she had lain for more than 30 years and nearly three months later it was announced that human remains had been recovered. One of England's most respected record-breakers

Above and below: Donald Campbell and his boat Bluebird pictured crashing at Coniston Water in the Lake District.

was finally laid to rest in Coniston on 12 September 2001.

No-hoper Foinavon wins Grand National

Named after a Scottish mountain by the Duchess of Westminster, racehorse Foinavon's jumping ability was so poor that he was soon sold and ended up at John Kempton's yard. He was entered into the 1967 Aintree Grand National and began the race with odds of 100-1.

Replacement jockey John Buckingham was called in to ride the big race because his trainer – who also doubled as his jockey – could not make the 10 stone weight. He could not have believed his luck when a couple of riderless horses brought down most of the field at the 23rd fence and Foinavon, far enough behind to avoid the pile-up, was the only horse to clear the obstacle at the first attempt.

Although around 17 jockeys remounted, they could not catch Foinavon who romped home 15 lengths ahead of favourite Honey End and 1968 Grand National winner Red Alligator in third.

Foinavon did run in the following year's race but he failed to negotiate the water jump and the 7th/23rd fence has since been renamed in honour of the 100-1 shot whose dream came true in 1967.

Above: Foinavon the 100-1 winner of the 1967 Grand National.

1960 1961 1962 1963 1964 1965 1966 1967 1968 1969

away leg against Vojvodina, returning from Yugoslavia with a 1-0 deficit. A dramatic second leg followed with Celtic taking almost an hour to equalise and it was Chalmers who kept up his record of scoring in every round. It fell to captain Billy McNeill to score the decisive second goal, heading home Charlie Gallagher's corner.

Dukla Prague were despatched 3-1 (two for Willie Wallace and one for Jimmy Johnstone) in the first leg of the semi-final so Celtic just needed to avoid a disastrous trip to Czechoslovakia to book their place in the Final. This they duly obliged with a 0-0 draw.

Celtic win European Cup

Scottish clubs played an integral part in 1967 European football competitions. Kilmarnock lost to Leeds in the semi-final of the Intercities Fairs Cup, Rangers lost to Bayern Munich in the Cup Winners' Cup Final but it was Celtic's Lisbon Lions who put Scotland on the European map in terms of club football.

FC Zurich were their first round opposition and goals from Tommy Gemmell and Joe McBride gave Celtic a 2-0 advantage to take to Switzerland. Jock Stein's side powered their way to a 3-0 victory, Gemmell scoring another two with one from Steve Chalmers, to set up a second round meeting with French Champions Nantes.

Both home and away legs finished 3-1 to the Bhoys with Chalmers and Bobby Lennox both scoring in each game. Celtic suffered their only defeat in the third round

Above: Billy McNeill of Celtic receives the European Cup trophy from the President of Portugal after the Scottish side's 2-1 victory over Inter Milan in Lisbon.

Celtic went into the Final in Lisbon against Inter Milan on a high after a domestic clean sweep of League, FA Cup and League Cup. After seven minutes, Inter were awarded a penalty which Mazzola converted to put the Italians in front, but goals from Gemmell (63 minutes) and Chalmers (85 minutes) ensured that Celtic went into the record books as the first British club to win the European Cup.

POLITICS & CURRENT AFFAIRS

Six Day War

The long running Arab-Israeli conflict is one of the saddest aspects of twentieth and twenty-first century history. The State of Israel was formed in 1948, following Nazi atrocities against Jews before and during World War Two, and was thought of by the western world as some sort of recompense for all the suffering incurred. Nearby Arab nations were however horrified that the Jews should be given a homeland in Palestine, which they too considered to be their homeland, and there was trouble from the very start.

The Arab countries – in particular Egypt, led by President Nasser – refused to recognise the new Jewish state, and Arab nationalists called for its destruction. In the years prior to 1967, Palestine fedayeen (guerrillas) mounted attacks on Israeli troops and civilians on Jewish territory, with Israel responding by mounting their own attacks on territory belonging to the Arabs. During 1967 the Arab states, led by Nasser, surrounded Israel and mobilised for war. On 5 June Israel launched a pre-emptive strike and began an attack which came to be known as the Six Day War, or the June War. In the space of less than a week, Israel drove the Arabs from the strategically important areas of the Sinai Peninsula, the Gaza Strip, the West Bank and the Golan Heights. While it was about it, Israel also re-united Jerusalem, the eastern part of which had been controlled by Jordan since 1949.

*1960 1961 1962 1963 1964 1965 1966 **1967** 1968 1969*

***Middle and below:** Advancing Israeli troops passing the wreckage of an enemy aeroplane near El Arish airport during the Six Day War and an Israeli tank churns up dust on the Golan Heights.*

REMEMBER THE SIXTIES

In a military sense, the war was a great success as far as Israel was concerned. Yet continued occupation of the territories taken in the Six Day War, and the building of Jewish settlements, have been a source of dispute ever since. One can only hope that one day reason will prevail, and that some sort of amicable solution may be found.

The pound in your pocket

By 1967 Prime Minister Harold Wilson was having a pretty tough time of it on the economic front. It was all going horribly wrong, with conflict in the Middle East, the closure of the Suez Canal and dock strikes all putting tremendous pressure on sterling. Wilson had inherited a deficit in the region of £800 million from the Conservative administration and he had, somehow,

managed to reduce it slightly, but an economic crisis was nevertheless looming.

The pound was linked to the US dollar, and Wilson decided that the British currency would have to be devalued. Accordingly, in November 1967, he announced that the exchange rate would be lowered from $2.80 to $2.40 to the pound. This represented a cut in the pound's value of 14.3% in relation to all major currencies. As so often happens when politicians make statements which are only half-true, Wilson's explanation of the devaluation led to widespread criticism. Presumably in an effort to make the meaning of the decision clear to those who were not well versed in economic theory, he said: 'It does not mean that the pound here in Britain, in your pocket or purse or in your bank, has been devalued.'

He went on to talk of tackling the country's economic problems, but the public relations damage had been done: everyone knew that prices would rise and that there were hard times just around the corner, and the press naturally proceeded to give the PM a hard time.

The opposition also had a field day, with Conservative leader Edward Heath accusing the government of failing to safeguard the value of the country's

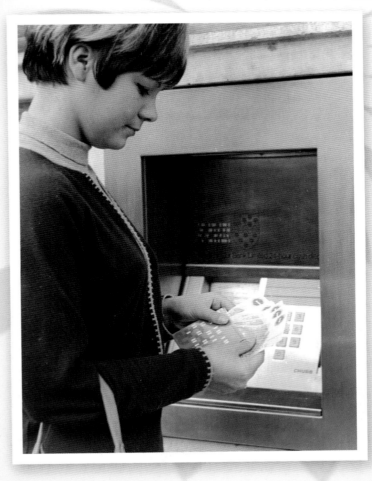

Above: A customer counts her 'devalued' money after using one of the world's first cashpoint machines.

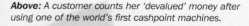

Breathe into this bag, Sir

When motorcars were first produced early in the twentieth century, few people could afford them. This remained the case until after the Second World War, but then car ownership took off. It was always known that 'driving under the influence' was dangerous but, with few cars on the road, a blind eye was largely turned towards the drunken motorist.

By the 1960s however, it was clear that drink-driving was becoming a problem. As early as 1954, the United States had introduced a 'breathalyser' to measure the amount of alcohol present in drivers suspected of the offence, and it was now time to introduce a similar device to Britain. A legal limit of 80 mg of alcohol per 100 ml of blood was decided upon, and the breathalyser, backed up by blood tests, began to be used in October 1967. Never again would a friendly bobby advise a motorist to 'drive home carefully, Sir', when the motorist was obviously as inebriated as a newt.

money, and reminding Wilson that Labour had continually promised not to devalue. The move was in part the cause of the defeat of the Labour government three years later.

1967

Above and below: A volunteer taking Britain's first breathalyser test and a policeman checking the crystal reading of one of the newly introduced tests.

1968

FASHION, CULTURE & ENTERTAINMENT

The opening of *Yellow Submarine, Hair, Oliver* and *Joseph*

Yellow Submarine, an animated film written by Lee Minoff based on the original 1966 song by the Beatles, was released at the height of psychedelic pop culture on 6 June 1968. It became a box-office hit due to its soundtrack from the Beatles and its creative images.

The music takes precedence over the plot and most of the film is a series of set-pieces designed to present the band's music, in a style reminiscent of Disney's

Selections by the Beatles plus original film m

Fantasia. It was written as a modern-day fairy tale that incorporated the ideals of the 'love' culture.

The US hippie musical *Hair* opened in New York in December 1967, but did not reach London until the following year due to anger over nudity, drug-taking and desecration of the American flag due to the show's strong anti-war message at the height of the Vietnam conflict. Written by two

Above: Child actors Jack Wild (left) and Mark Lester, who play the Artful Dodger and Oliver Twist in the musical 'Oliver!'
Below: 'Yellow Submarine' album cover.

out of work actors, Gerome Ragni and James Rado, the show was billed as an American tribal love-rock musical and opened in the UK one day after the abolition of the Lord Chamberlain's powers of theatre censorship which dated back to 1737. Director Tom O'Horgan, responsible for the London production, felt that attitudes to the show's nudity were greatly over-emphasised.

In contrast to *Hair*, *Oliver* the stage musical received rave reviews and was adapted for film by Lionel Bart and Vernon Harris. Directed by Sir Carol Reed, uncle of Oliver Reed who played Bill Sykes in the 1968 production, it was hailed as one of the few films that is better than the original play on which it was based.

Bill Sykes's songs were removed from the film version so that Oliver Reed could make his character more frightening as Charles Dickens, author of the book, *Oliver Twist*, on which both versions are based, had intended.

The cast for the film included, Ron Moody (Fagin), Harry Secombe (Mr Bumble), Shani Wallis (Nancy), Mark Lester (Oliver) and Jack Wild as the Artful Dodger.

Joseph And The Amazing Technicolor Dreamcoat was the second musical written by Andrew Lloyd Webber and Tim Rice. Light-hearted in style, it was first presented at the Colet Court School in London on 1 March 1968.

Lasting 20 minutes, the show had been commissioned by the head of music at the school and both the orchestra and singers consisted of pupils of the school. Two months' later, the school gave a second performance at Central Hall, Westminster and received a review from *The Sunday Times* before giving a third performance at St Paul's Cathedral in November that same year.

The following year, Lloyd Webber and Rice decided to release an album of the show, but it did not do well until the duo released the music to *Jesus Christ Superstar*. Frank Dunlop finally produced *Joseph*, based on the biblical story, at a professional level in 1972. Success led the show to Broadway in 1982.

Below: Andrew Lloyd Webber (left) with his writing partner and lyricist Tim Rice.

1968 1967 1966 1965 1964 1963 1962 1961 1960

Vidal Sassoon

Vidal Sassoon was a key force in the 1960s for the commercial direction of hair styling and was instrumental in turning the profession into a multi-million dollar industry. He is the father of the modernist style and, by 1968, was one of the most prolific and influential hair stylists of the decade.

Born in London on 17 January 1928 to Jewish parents, he specialised in styles that were modern and low maintenance. He was a protégé of Raymond Bessone, also known as Mr Teazy-Weezy, who owned a salon in Mayfair, London, and had a long list of celebrity clients.

Sassoon's own famous clients included Mary Quant, Jean Shrimpton and Mia Farrow, who famously flew him to the US when she wanted her hair styled for the film *Rosemary's Baby* at a cost of $5,000.

He was responsible for the geometric style and the wash-and-wear perm, although he preferred the natural shine of hair for effect and did not use hair-sprays or lacquers. In 1963, he created a short, angular hairstyle cut on a horizontal plane which recreated the classic 'bob'. By the early 1980s, Vidal Sassoon had sold his name to manufacturers of hair-care products and multinational Procter & Gamble applied the name to shampoos and conditioners worldwide.

In 2002 Vidal Sassoon salons were sold to Regis Corporation, he cut his ties with Procter & Gamble two years later and is no longer associated with the brand that bears his

name. Vidal Sassoon fought for the Israeli Army when the State of Israel was declared which led to Muslims and Arabs refusing to purchase his products. He was also a member of the British Anti-Fascist organisation, the 43 Group.

Above: Jane Fonda in one of the futuristic outfits from 'Barbarella'.
Below: Mia Farrow having her blonde hair cut short by Vidal Sassoon.

REMEMBER THE SIXTIES

Space-age Fashions

In 1967, designer Jaques Fonteray copied the space-age fashions of French designers Pierre Cardin and Andre Courrèges from the earlier 1960s for Jane Fonda's costumes in *Barbarella.* His futuristic outfits, coupled with mass hysteria over the imminent moon landings, ensured that 1968 was the year that the look really took off.

Pierre had designed a number of futuristic fashions including space-age cat suits and body stockings. He launched his space-age collection in 1964 where some outfits were made entirely from metal and plastic. Female models were dressed in shiny vinyl, high-legged leather boots and space helmets. Meanwhile, Courrèges's collections featured silver and white PVC with bonded seams, silver PVC 'moongirl' pants, white catsuits and monochrome mini skirts and dresses.

The first decimal coins come into circulation

On 23 April 1968, the first decimal coins made their way into purses and wallets throughout Britain in preparation for replacing the then current system of pounds, shillings and pence.

Five and ten pence pieces were designed to the same size, weight and value as shillings and florins but, as confusion reigned on the high street, many shoppers refused to take them. Many thought the new five pence piece was worth five old pennies while in fact it was actually worth a shilling i.e. 12 old pence.

Pictures of the new coins were placed in newspapers to give consumers some idea about what to expect ahead of the formal decimalisation planned for 1971. At some larger stores in London special training was given to staff prior to the arrival of the new coins.

However, chairman of the Decimal Currency Board, Lord Fiske, warned that price tags would remain in old money for a time to avoid too much confusion and that the new coins would be in the minority in people's change from tills for a long time.

Conversion to decimal currency with the new system of 100 new pence to the pound continued gradually over three years and culminated in 'Decimal Day' on 15 February 1971. After the first new coins it would be the 50 pence piece that made its debut, replacing the 10 shilling note.

Above: A complete set of the new decimal currency showing the reverse design of the five denominations and the obverse design, common to all.

Hawaii-Five-O

Created by Leonard Freeman in 1968, the television series *Hawaii-Five-O* was set in Hawaii where plots centred on an elite branch of the Hawaii state police. Answerable only to the Governor of Hawaii, and headed by Steve McGarrett (played by Jack Lord), the team worked with the Honolulu police to fight the underworld in the island state. *Hawaii-Five-O*'s mission was to deal with organised crime, murder, assassinations and any other major felonies.

Ex-Navy Intelligence investigator McGarrett is a tough Irish cop with a determined nature. He worked alongside second in command Dan Williams 'Dan-O' (James MacArthur), Chin Ho Kelly (Kam Fong), Kono (Zulu) Duke Lukela (Herman Wedemeyer all Hawaiian natives) and Ben Kokua (Al Harrington). The arch-

enemy was Wo Fat, a Chinese agent whose plans were always thwarted by McGarrett and his team, but who also managed to avoid arrest.

MUSIC

February

Beatles George Harrison and John Lennon, along with partners Patti and Cynthia, this month took time out to travel to the banks of the Ganges in India and seek 'absolute bliss consciousness' with their favourite guru, the Maharishi Mahesh Yogi. Ringo and Maureen Starr, Paul McCartney and girlfriend Jane Asher, American actress Mia Farrow and folk-singer Donovan joined them three days later. But harmony proved short-lived: the Stars returned before the allotted fortnight was over, reportedly complaining about the 'spicy food' on offer.

Above: Jack Lord next to two women in bikinis – in a still from the television show, 'Hawaii Five-O'.
Below: The Maharishi Mahesh Yogi.

Then a young nurse from California complained of sexual advances from the Maharishi, who'd also apparently belied his non-materialistic nature by demanding a substantial fee to be filmed. When John and George confronted him, they didn't receive the answers they wanted, and left the ashram. In June, the Beatles would renounce the Maharishi at a New York press conference, Paul admitting that 'we made a mistake... he's human. We thought at first that he wasn't.' The allegedly less than wholly holy man was also the subject of Lennon's satirical 'Sexy Sadie' which appeared on the 'The Beatles' double (White) album, its title changed from 'Maharishi' for legal reasons.

Ratifying weeks of rumour, composer, singer and guitarist Syd Barrett, Pink Floyd's biggest asset and biggest liability, left the group which, early the previous month, had enlisted a second guitarist, Dave Gilmour, initially, to keep pace with and anchor a drug-addled and increasingly unreliable Barrett's creative input on stage and in the studio. However, it soon made more sense for Dave, better equipped to deal with the demands of rock stardom, to replace Syd altogether.

Endeavouring to master his inner chaos, Barrett managed two solo albums before retiring as a professional musician. The once-charismatic Syd, now as tubbily middle-aged as his former bandmates and a shadowy, reclusive figure, remained a source of

Below: The Beatles and friends in audience to the Maharishi Mahesh Yogi.

1968

1967

1966

1965

1964

1963

1962

1961

1960

fascination to fans until his death in 2006, as well as record company moguls who continue to scrape the barrel for anything on which he so much as breathed back in the days of 'See Emily Play' when he was a slim-hipped, wild-haired profile defined by a *Top Of The Pops* arc-light.

September

The Bee Gees – the Brothers Gibb – topped the British charts this month and scored their biggest US hit thus far with 'I've Gotta Get A Message To You' – about a condemned man one hour from execution. 'Beautiful sadness' was very much part of the outfit's emotional vocabulary in the late 1960s when the sepulchral echo of a recording complex's twisting metal staircase, and news of the children buried alive by a shifting slag heap in Aberfan in 1966 combined to inspire 'New York Mining Disaster 1941', the contemplations of a pitman trapped by a subterranean landslide.

Aided by much media build-up, this catapulted the Bee Gees into the UK Top 20 for the first time. Barry, Maurice and Robin Gibb had, however, been famous in Australia since the early 1960s when the brilliantined, toothy trio had appeared regularly on the nationwide pop series *Bandstand*. After a period as Beatle-like moptops, they stumbled upon their own sound, had domestic hits and, after recruiting a drummer and lead guitarist, were brought to London to be groomed for the Big Time by another Australian, Robert Stigwood, whose agency had just merged with Brian Epstein's NEMS organisation.

Success was immediate, but internal squabbles reduced the group briefly to only Barry and Maurice before Robin rejoined after a solo smash, 1969's 'Saved By The Bell'. Backed by session players, the siblings made the first of umpteen comebacks with 'How Do You Mend A Broken Heart', a US million-seller. Another slack period precipitated a shift towards disco,

which paid sufficient dividends, especially with the *Saturday Night Fever* film soundtrack and its singles, for the three to coast through the next decade. Yet, just to show they could, they knocked out the first of more major hits with 'You Win Again' in 1987.

In 2001, the Bee Gees completed their final recordings and stage performances under the old regime – because Maurice was to die suddenly three years later. Since then, Barry and Robin have been preoccupied with individual projects, though they reunited in 2006 for two all-star charity spectaculars.

The last date – in Bournemouth – of Roy Orbison's six-week British tour was cancelled as the singer was

Above: The Bee Gees posing on a balcony, (left to right) Barry Gibb, Maurice Gibb, drummer Colin Peterson, Robin Gibb and bassist Vince Melouney.

the entire house ablaze. By the time Roy arrived, however, most of the fire engines had gone.

The flame-ravaged site was sold to Johnny Cash, who grew an orchard there – and Orbison coped, as he'd done two years earlier when his wife died in a road accident, by burying himself in work, even as his hits dried up. While his concerts were buoyed by past triumphs, he steered clear of nostalgia revues and continued to release new material. This paid off with a chart comeback and membership of the Traveling

flying home to Nashville, fuzzy with an injected sedative to dull the pain of tragic family news. His two elder sons, Duane and Tony, had been messing about in the basement where petrol was stored for their father's collection of antique cars. An explosion down there killed both boys and set

Below: Roy Orbison poses with his Rolls Royce.

Wilburys 'supergroup' with George Harrison, Bob Dylan, Jeff Lynne and Tom Petty just prior to the ill-starred Roy's fatal heart attack in December 1988.

November

In an interview with *Beat Instrumental*, drummer Ginger Baker confirmed the calculated disbandment of Cream, the London-based group he'd formed in 1966 with guitarist Eric Clapton from John Mayall's Bluesbreakers and, on bass, Jack Bruce, late of Manfred Mann. Bruce agreed to undertake the bulk of the singing only after other possibilities had been investigated. Baker, for example, gave first refusal to Ray Phillips of the Nashville Teens. A similar invitation to

the Spencer Davis Group's Steve Winwood fell on stonier ground – though, unlike Ray, Steve had no qualms about misplaced loyalty as he was already assembling what was to be Traffic.

Cream's intention expressed during rehearsals in a suburban scout hut had been to play the blues in Home Counties clubland. Yet they were not quite so humble two years later with a double album, 'Wheels Of Fire', going gold across the Atlantic where collegiate youth seemed fair game to buy anything British labelled 'heavy', 'progressive' or 'blues'. Their very name implied virtuosity, and 23-year-old Eric was deified as a guitar hero, even as Cream's playing stagnated into 'endless, meaningless solos,' grimaced Clapton, 'We were not indulging ourselves so much as our audiences –

Above: Cream – Jack Bruce, Ginger Baker and Eric Clapton.
Below: Clapton is interviewed by the press.

because that's what they wanted.' As long as such customers roared indiscriminate ovations for both strings of bum notes and the trio's most startling moments, Cream broke box-office records in Uncle Sam's baseball parks and concrete coliseums.

Yet, for old time's sake, their final recital was staged at London's Royal Albert Hall on 26 November. The set included their usual triple-forte work-out of Willie Dixon's 'Spoonful', cut, dried and dissected to nigh on twenty minutes to snowblinded applause. A more measured and succinct arrangement cropped up when a reformed Cream booked the same venue for four concerts in May 2005, doing the same at New York's Madison Square Garden the following October.

SPORT

Mexico City Olympics

The 1968 Summer Olympics will be remembered for numerous reasons, including the Black Power salute given by some American athletes and Dick Fosbury's new approach to the high jump.

These Games saw the introduction of sex testing for women, drug testing for all winners. For the first time the electronic timing was taken as the official record and a synthetic material was used on the athletics track.

Sprinters Tommie Smith and John Carlos – winners of the 200 metres gold and bronze respectively – bowed their heads and gave a clenched-fist salute in protest over racism in America…they were immediately thrown off the team.

American high jumper Dick Fosbury had begun experimenting with a new technique where the jumper goes over the bar head first and backwards – now known as the Fosbury Flop – five years earlier. This time round he set an Olympic and American record with his jump of 2.24 metres.

139

Above: America's Richard Fosbury wins the gold medal in the high jump at the Mexico City Olympics.
Below: American athlete Bob Beamon breaks the long jump record at the 1968 Olympics.

1960 1961 1962 1963 1964 1965 1966 1967 **1968** 1969

1968

1960 1961 1962 1963 1964 1965 1966 1967 1968 1969

There had been concern expressed regarding Mexico City's 7,349 feet altitude but the black American sprinters flourished, winning all but one event under 800 metres in or near a world record time. Englishman David Hemery spoiled the US clean sweep, a world record time of 48.10 seconds giving him the 400 metres hurdles gold medal.

Bob Beaman's long jump record of 8.90 metres, beating the previous record by a massive two feet, was predicted to stand until the twenty-first century…it eventually fell to fellow American Mike Powell's 8.95 metre leap in 1991. Another notable performance was by Al Oerter who won his fourth consecutive discus gold.

Other British success stories were few and far between: Christopher Finnegan won the middleweight boxing title, Margitta Gummel won the women's shotput gold, John Braithwaite won the clay pigeon shooting and the Great Britain team claimed the Flying Dutchman yachting and horseriding's three-day eventing titles.

Man Utd win European Cup

A decade after the Munich air disaster had decimated Matt Busby's young team, Manchester United became the first English club to win football's European Cup.

The campaign kicked off ties against Maltese minnows Hibernians (4-0 aggregate) and Sarajevo (2-1) with Polish Champions Gornik Zabrze their quarter-final opponents in a physical encounter. Centre-half Florenski scored an own goal with an attempted interception before a last-minute strike by youngster Brian Kidd gave United a 2-0 advantage. They lost the return leg 1-0 on a pitch covered by so much snow that it was difficult to see the markings.

The first leg of the semi-final saw Old Trafford play host to the mighty Real Madrid, who had won the title six times in the 12 years it had been in existence. George Best scored the only goal of the game and set up a nail-biting return at the Bernabeu.

By half-time, United were 3-1 down and heading out with only a Zoco own goal to show for their efforts. They fought back and levelled the aggregate score through David Sadler with 15 minutes to go. The unlikely hero was defender Bill Foulkes who scored the winner five minutes later to book a trip to Wembley (he only scored nine goals in more than 700 appearances for the club).

The first half passed without incident – Eusebio went closest when he hit United's crossbar – and eight

Above: George Best grins in the background as his Manchester United team mate David Sadler lifts the European Cup.

minutes after the break, Bobby Charlton broke the deadlock with a glancing header. With just nine minutes to go, Jaime Graca scored an equaliser to send the game into extra time. Three goals in five minutes from Best, Kidd (on his nineteenth birthday) and Charlton sealed United's victory and brought the trophy back to Old Trafford for the first time in the club's history.

Jim Clark dies during a Formula 2 race in Germany

With two Formula 1 world titles (in 1963 and 1965) under his belt, James 'Jim' Clark – born in Scotland on 4 March 1936 – was favourite for the 1968 motor-racing Championship and his partnership with Graham Hill in the Lotus team was flourishing.

His climb to the top has been astounding and, despite witnessing tragedies early in his career (including the death of two drivers at Belgium in 1960 and of another driver and 14 spectators following a collision involving Clark at Monza a year later), he came to be hailed as the greatest driver of his era.

An oil leak in the last race of the 1964 season deprived him of the chance to take a hat-trick of titles but he broke the legendary Juan Manuel Fangio's record by registering his 25th career Grand Prix win in South Africa in the first event of 1968. On 7 April 1968, however, he was killed when his Lotus suffered a tyre failure in a Formula 2 race at Hockenheim in Germany.

1960 1961 1962 1963 1964 1965 1966 1967 **1968** 1969

Below: Jim Clark with the Lotus team.

REMEMBER THE SIXTIES

1969 1969 1968 1967 1966 1965 1964 1963 1962 1961 1960

POLITICS & CURRENT AFFAIRS

Year of unrest

1968 was a year of unrest across Europe. Students across the continent, encouraged by radical lecturers and teachers, started to express their discontent with the modern world and to call for change. In May, France was more or less paralysed by a general strike which followed student riots. The students had started by calling for reform of the 'bourgeois university system',

and were later joined by workers protesting about poor state salaries and just about everything else. The riots culminated in a march of an estimated 800,000 people and a strike affected the whole of France. At one stage, tanks were placed on the outskirts of Paris to prevent a possible full-scale revolution. President de Gaulle was not amused, but he did eventually introduce reforms to calm the situation.

During the summer the Northern Ireland civil rights movement became established, with Catholics marching and demonstrating against discrimination in

Below: A street riot in Paris, initiated by the students of the University of Paris in protest against police brutality.

started by that country's leader, Alexander Dubcek. The so called 'Prague Spring' was soon turned into autumnal depression, as 200,000 Warsaw Pact soldiers invaded the country to restore communist order – for a few years, at least. Dubcek and his colleagues were summoned to Moscow, where they were forced to agree to the re-introduction of the status quo. Hungary had rebelled against Soviet domination in 1956 and this, together with the events in Prague in 1968, signalled the eventual collapse of Soviet communism. The collapse would not, however, occur for a good few years yet.

Assassination of Martin Luther King

Martin Luther King, the son and grandson of Baptist pastors, was the leading figure in the American civil rights campaign during the 1950s and 1960s. King had attended segregated schools before going on to gain a degree at Morehouse College, a well-known institution for black students. He later gained another degree at Boston University.

King's first act as a civil rights campaigner was to organise a 'bus boycott'. He was arrested, but after 1956 blacks and whites were free to ride on buses without segregation. Martin Luther King was to be arrested many times during his short life, and he

jobs and housing. Troubled times had never really gone away in the province, but now they were back with a vengeance. It would all become a lot worse in the years which followed.

Meanwhile, in August, Soviet tanks entered Prague to halt the march towards reform in Czechoslovakia, which had been

Above: Martin Luther King speaks at a press conference

1968

64 1965 1966 1967 1968

960 1961 1962 19

was to survive several assassination attempts. He wrote a number of books and many articles advocating non-violent action and, in 1963, he made his famous 'I have a dream' speech on the steps of the Lincoln Memorial in Washington, before an audience of 250,000.

King was awarded the Nobel Peace Prize in 1964. By then, his campaign had brought about many changes for black people in American society, although there was still a very long way to go. His life was cut short by an assassin's bullet on 4 April 1968, as he stood on a hotel balcony in Memphis. News of Martin Luther King's death at the age of 39 years shocked the world. US President Lyndon Johnson said: 'I ask every citizen to reject the blind violence that has taken Dr. King, who lived by non-violence.'

James Earl Ray confessed to King's murder and was sentenced to 99 years in jail. He later retracted his confession, saying that he had played only a minor part in a murder conspiracy. Some believed that the US Government was behind the assassination, but no compelling evidence was ever found. Ray died in prison in 1998.

Bobby Kennedy assassinated

Bobby Kennedy was scheduled to be the USA's second President Kennedy, but he never made it. He was gunned down on 5 June 1968 at the Ambassador Hotel in Los Angeles, shortly after winning the California Primary. Kennedy was on his way from the hotel's ballroom to give a press conference. Somewhat strangely, his planned route took him through the

Above: *Martin Luther King lying in state – Memphis, Tennessee, as his colleagues pay their respects to him.*

hotel's pantry. Sirhan Sirhan, a Palestinian Arab, who fired a .22 revolver at Kennedy, was arrested and later found guilty of murder. Initially sentenced to death, Sirhan's sentence was later commuted to life imprisonment.

Doubts were soon cast on Sirhan Sirhan's guilt. It seems certain that other people also fired shots, and it is thought a bullet from another gun may have actually killed Kennedy. As usual, accusations of a cover-up came thick and fast. What is certain is that the curse of the Kennedys had struck once more. When he was gunned down, Bobby Kennedy was 42 years old.

1960 1961 1962 1963 1964 1965 1966 1967 **1968** 1969

Above and below: Robert F Kennedy speaking at a rally during his campaign for US president and mourners at the British Embassy pay their respects.

1960 1961 1962 1963 1964 1965 1966 1967 1968 1969

1969

FASHION, CULTURE & ENTERTAINMENT

Space introduces the first moon landing and *Star Trek*

On 25 May 1961 in a speech to Congress, President Kennedy expressed his concerns that the US was falling behind the Soviet Union in the technology race. He challenged his nation to put a man on the moon by the end of the decade.

President Kennedy would not live to see a man on the moon, but his country did indeed rise to the challenge and, on 16 July 1969, *Apollo 11* was

launched from the US Kennedy Space Centre. The astronauts on board were Commander Neil Armstrong, command module pilot Michael Collins and lunar module pilot Edwin E ('Buzz') Aldrin Jr.

At 4.17 p.m. on 20 July 1969, with less than 30 seconds' worth of fuel left, Commander Neil Armstrong safely landed on the moon with his crew. Armstrong left the

Above: The Apollo Lunar Module known as the Eagle descends onto the surface of the moon.
Below: Edwin 'Buzz' Aldrin walks on the surface of the moon during the Apollo 11 mission.

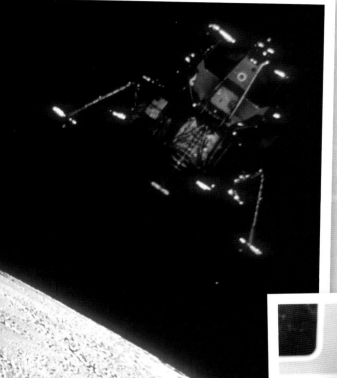

television series (of 726 episodes), ten feature films, hundreds of novels, computer and video games all of which are set within the same fictional universe created by Gene Roddenberry, a former policeman and pilot who joined the US Army Air Corps in 1941.

Star Trek is based on optimism where humanity has united with other intelligent species in the galaxy. The central characters are devoted to discovering new worlds and civilisations while promoting peace and understanding. The plots involved in the early television series allegorize the politics of the time and, because many of those issues still linger, it probably explains the continuing popularity of *Star Trek* and the interest of all those fans known as 'Trekkies'.

lunar module (named *Eagle*) and stepped onto the moon's surface – the first man ever to do so – where he was joined by Aldrin. They spent 21 hours on the lunar surface and returned to the command module, where Collins was patiently orbiting the moon, with 46 pounds of lunar rocks. *Apollo 11* completed its mission and the three-man crew were safely returned to earth on 24 July. President Kennedy's wish had been accomplished.

In the same month, *Star Trek*, a unique television series, first aired on UK television. It went on to become a science-fiction franchise spanning six

1960 1961 1962 1963 1964 1965 1966 1967 1968 **1969**

Below: William Shatner as Captain Kirk, DeForest Kelley as Dr 'Bones' McCoy and Leonard Nimoy as Mr Spock in the television series 'Star Trek'.

1969 1968 1967 1966 1965 1964 1963 1962 1961 1960

Judy Garland dies aged 47 years

Tragic actress and singer July Garland died of an accidental overdose of prescribed pills on 22 June 1969. She was 47. Despite mounting debts, a repossessed house, weight problems and depression, Garland had continued to perform right up until her death. This was all a far cry from the early days and heyday of a woman who started out as a child actor with no formal training and emerged as an iconic figure of showbusiness.

She was born Frances Ethel Gumm on 6 October 1922 and was the youngest of three daughters. Her father was a theatre manager and his youngest child made her singing debut at the age of two singing the chorus of 'Jingle Bells' in her father's movie palace. Judy teamed up with her two older sisters to form the Gumm Sisters. Their success was never realised and it was Judy who was often singled out for mention as the undisputed star of the trio.

Having changed her name to Garland at the suggestion of George Jessel, Judy auditioned for MGM in 1935. She made her first single 'Stompin' At The Savoy' with the Bing Crosby Orchestra, and it was released by Decca Records, with whom she also had a contract. As with all contract players, Garland was loaned to 20th Century Fox where she made her first feature film *Pigskin Parade* in 1936. Back at MGM she gave a rendition of 'You Made Me Love You' which was sung while Garland was holding a picture of MGM's leading man, Clark Gable.

Garland was paired in a leading role with Mickey Rooney for the first of many partnerships in

Below: Judy Garland performing on stage a few months before her death.

REMEMBER THE SIXTIES

Thoroughbreds Don't Cry (1937) and, as a teen starlet in the making, was picked by MGM for the part of Dorothy Gale in The Wizard Of Oz in 1939.

Garland's career was never in doubt from that moment on and as her professional life was on the ascent, her personal life spiralled into self-destruction – a route that would eventually destroy her.

The Italian Job

Written by Troy Kennedy Martin and directed by Peter Collinson, The

Caine plays dapper mobster Charlie Croker who stages a gold bullion robbery in Turin while Noel Coward, in the role of Mr Bridger, is an incarcerated criminal mastermind who runs a gangland empire from his prison cell. Croker wants to sabotage the traffic-control computer and escape in Mini Cooper sports cars along a planned route. Other roles in the film are played by Benny Hill and Robert Powell.

Italian Job was a comedy caper film starring Michael Caine released in 1969. Such was its success with UK audiences that it became a national institution and quickly picked up a cult following.

The action is set in London and Turin and reflects the swinging Sixties. The film gives a light-hearted view of London criminal activities which was far from the truth and Caine later revealed that he took the part in

Above: Michael Caine star of 'The Italian Job'.
Below: A scene from the robbery in the film 'The Italian Job'.

1971's *Get Carter* in order to show the brutal realism of organised crime in the capital.

Biba

Innovative designer Barbara Hulanicki was just as interested in pioneering clothes that were affordable as Mary Quant. Like Quant, she recognised the needs of the youth market and came up with an innovative way to cater for them by creating Biba, a postal-boutique operation which she set up with her husband, Stephen Fitz-Simon, in 1963. The philosophy promoted was, 'knock-down, throw-away-and-buy-another' and, after

opened a couple of small boutiques not long after and the stores proved very popular. Designed like discos with dark mahogany screens and rock music blaring, Hulanicki sold her knock-down clothing with designs in her own fabrics.

Biba Ltd was launched in 1969, with Dorothy Perkins becoming the largest shareholder. A store on Kensington High Street opened

coverage in *The Mirror* newspaper (May 1964) of a Biba gingham dress costing under £3.00, orders flooded in and 17,000 dresses were sold.

In 1968, the first Biba mail-order catalogue was launched and a further five catalogues were published before it was wound-up in 1969. Customers were encouraged to come in and try anything on when Biba

in 1969 selling the company brand of clothes, make-up and other accessories, but closed its doors in September 1975.

Free Love and Woodstock

The music festival Woodstock took place between 15-17 August 1969, representing the counter-culture of

Above: A music fan at Woodstock pop festival in his car covered in anti-war slogans for love and peace.
Below: Fashion designer and proprietor of Biba boutiques, Barbara Hulanicki.

from the festival, but sales of two albums and the 1970 documentary film of the same name helped the event to eventually become profitable. The promoters had come up with the slogan 'Three days of Peace and Music' designed to placate suspicious local officials while appealing to the anti-war sentiment.

MUSIC

March

When his ritualised cavortings on the boards brought the Doors much notoriety, singer Jim Morrison did not disappoint at a show in Miami's Dinner Key auditorium which ended with his arrest for indecency.

the 1960s and the ultimate climax of the hippie era. The event was staged some 40 miles south-west of Woodstock itself when Sam Yasgur persuaded his father to let the event go ahead on their farmland in Sullivan County.

Originally planned to be held in Woodstock, hence the name, the event attracted more than 500,000 people and roads were jammed with traffic. Many abandoned their cars and walked for miles to the festival. Many locals gave food and blankets to concert-goers and while facilites were overcrowded, many people shared their food, alcohol and drugs.

The stars of Woodstock were the Who and Jimi Hendrix, while Joni Mitchell's song 'Woodstock' became a major hit, even though she was unable to attend the event. Initially no profits were made (despite setting out to)

Below: Group photo of 'The Doors'.

REMEMBER THE SIXTIES

The trouble started when technical problems caused 'Touch Me' – the latest hit single – to expire in mid-verse. Then scattered booing launched Morrison into what organist Ray Manzarek would describe as a send-up of his sex-symbol status with a routine involving a towel. In the process, he may have exposed himself inadvertently for a split-second, but backstage opinion intimated that the resulting accusations were fabricated by parochial authorities, keen to strike a blow against this anti-establishment icon.

An attempt to avoid prosecution by flying back to Los Angeles was thwarted by Morrison's detention by the FBI on landing. While he awaited trial, all Doors bookings over the next five months were cancelled, and later ones threatened with instant closure at the remotest hint of an unbuttoned fly.

Weeping female fans mobbed London's Marylebone Registry Office on that dark March morning when Paul McCartney and North American photographer Linda Eastman tied the knot. Next, the marriage was blessed in Paul's local church in St John's Wood. To limit the chances of an outbreak of Beatlemania, none of the other members of a fragmenting group showed up at either building, and a raid by a police drug squad on George Harrison's Weybridge home prevented his attendance at the reception.

A week later, John Lennon smoked a cigarette during a much quieter wedding to Japanese-American artist Yoko Ono at the British Consulate in Gibraltar. It was followed by a 'Bed-In For Peace' at the Amsterdam Hilton's honeymoon suite. The happy couple hoped that lying about for a week while entertaining the press would stop the atrocities in Biafra and Vietnam more effectively than any protest march or student sit-in.

Below: Paul McCartney weds Linda Eastman. With them is daughter Heather.
Below right: John Lennon and Yoko Ono with their marriage certificate after their wedding in Gibraltar.

Both the ceremony and the Bed-In would be mentioned in 'The Ballad Of John And Yoko', the Beatles' final British Number 1.

June

Following the disbandment of both Traffic and Cream in autumn 1968, the press dropped hints of a collaboration between Eric Clapton and Steve Winwood. This proved to have substance as the two began rehearsals in Eric's Surrey mansion with Ginger Baker and bass guitarist Rick Grech (from Family). After naming themselves 'Blind Faith' – Eric's suggestion – wheels were set in motion for a recording contract, a US tour and, before that, a free concert in London's Hyde Park on a summer Saturday.

A crowd of around 150,000 – briefly the largest assembly for any cultural event accommodated by the capital – sat through a hot afternoon of Donovan, the rabble-rousing Edgar Broughton Band and other turns that preceded the main event. Yet, if anyone was expecting magic, Blind Faith delivered mere music. 'We weren't ready,' confessed Clapton, 'but we had no choice.' As well as overhauls of 'Under My Thumb' by the Rolling Stones and Buddy Holly's 'Well... All Right', the set embraced originals from the forthcoming eponymous album.

Only a miracle could have saved the mere mortals that were Blind Faith, but, determined to like both the show and the curate's egg of an LP, critics were kind about the smart-Alec instrumental intricacies and self-indulgent soloing that camouflaged nondescript songs in need of editing.

The group hit trouble in the States where they'd been heralded with banner headlines, a *Time* colour spread and foyer posters proclaiming the 'Ultimate Supergroup'. The antithesis of Hyde Park's relative tranquillity, *Rolling Stone* magazine's 'Acclamation By Riot!' was an accurate summary of US audience conduct: a near-ceaseless barrage of stamping, whistling, discomforted snarls and, worst of all, bawled requests for Cream and, to a lesser degree, Traffic's favourites. With some of these in the set and with amplifiers flat-out, Blind Faith threw in the towel at the Los Angeles Forum on 15 August. Within a day, the retinue had scattered – Clapton to record a solo album, Baker to form Airforce, a percussion-heavy big band with Grech on bass, and Winwood to try again with Traffic.

Above: Experimental psychedelic rock group Traffic, with founder member, the young multi-instrumentalist Stevie Winwood (bottom left).

1960 1961 1962 1963 1964 1965 1966 1967 1968 **1969**

REMEMBER THE SIXTIES

July

Even before leaving the Rolling Stones the previous month, Brian Jones had been sounding out other musicians about starting a new group. Among those who visited Cotchford Farm, his haven in the Sussex Weald, were personnel from the Jimi Hendrix Experience, the Crazy World Of Arthur Brown and the Jeff Beck Group. Jones was, however, unable to interest Ian Stewart, the Stones' pianist-cum-road manager. 'I formed one group with you,' explained Ian, 'and that was enough.'

In the small hours of Thursday 3 July, Stewart was the first Stone to be informed that, around midnight, Brian had drowned in the Cotchford Farm swimming pool. The midsummer humidity, his asthma, an intake of alcohol and drugs and oncoming drowsiness had all combined to bring about his body's final rebellion after a lifetime of violation.

For the Stones, the rest of the year would be, gloomed Keith Richards, 'tinged with black emotions. You were constantly being drawn into the vortex of black events.'

December

A free outdoor concert by the Rolling Stones at Altamont Speedway track near Livermore, California, that had been intended as a thank-you gesture to fans ended in tragedy when Hell's Angels who had been appointed as security guards to police the 300,000 crowd stabbed spectator Meredith Hunter.

The incident was later seen by millions in the Maysles Brothers film *Gimme Shelter*, and effectively brought the era of peace and love to a grisly end. Three more festival-goers met their

Above: Brian Jones, seen shortly before his death.
Below: The 15th Century farmhouse at Hartfield, Sussex owned by Brian Jones the morning after the musician was found dead in the swimming pool.

ends at an event acclaimed by *Rolling Stone* magazine beforehand as 'a little Woodstock...an *instant* Woodstock'; two were run over by cars as they lay in sleeping bags, while a third drowned in an irrigation ditch.

Keith Richards' considered verdict: 'One thing Altamont taught us was not to do anything like that again. In any case, rock sounds better in a room with 200 people.' Jagger: 'It was a nightmare, but at the time it was one of those 'ere we go, we've gotta get through it somehow' things because we couldn't just

leave.' Jagger had envisioned Altamont as 'thousands of people getting along and enjoying the music,' but after losing their original venue, Golden Gate Park, the concert organisers had to find a replacement, finally settling on Altamont. The result was a massive event involving hundreds of thousands of people that was essentially improvised.

Though the Stones – whose 14-strong entourage made a rapid post-gig exit in an eight-seat helicopter – are always associated with the incident which occurred while they were on stage,

the supporting bill included such un-Satanic attractions as Santana, Crosby Stills Nash and Young and the Flying Burrito Brothers. Altamont, an avoidable tragedy, has gone down in history as ending music's greatest decade with a dose of unpalatable reality.

SPORT

Ann Jones wins Wimbledon

One of Britain's most successful tennis players, Ann Jones became the first left-hander to win the women's title at Wimbledon on 4 July 1969. Even the Beatles apparently took a break from recording to listen to her exploits on the radio.

Born Adrianne Shirley Haydon in Birmingham on 7 October 1938, Jones (who married in 1962) had beaten (fifth seed) Nancy Richey and top seed Margaret Court en route to the Final. There she met Billie Jean King, winner of the title for the last three years and who

Above: American rock group Crosby, Stills, Nash, and Young who also performed with the Stones at Altamont.
Below: Ann Jones holds the Wimbledon trophy after her victory over Billie Jean King.

1960 1961 1962 1963 1964 1965 1966 1967 1968 1969

was unbeaten in 24 consecutive matches. Indeed, Jones had lost to King in the 1967 Wimbledon Final when, hampered by a leg injury, she ceded defeat by 11-9, 6-4.

This time, however, it was different and – despite losing the first set – it was Jones who triumphed 3-6, 6-3, 6-2 to the delight of the Centre Court audience. Britain now had its second female Wimbledon Champion since the Second World War. She rounded the tournament off with the mixed doubles title (with Australian Fred Stolle) and was later voted BBC Personality of the Year.

Her parents were outstanding table tennis players and Ann excelled in this sport as well, enjoying an international career between 1953-59. But it was in lawn tennis that she earned most success, beginning with the British Junior Championships in 1954 and 1955.

She reached the Final of the French Open five times, winning in 1961 and 1966. She also won three doubles titles in Paris (1963, 1968 and 1969). Ann reached two US Championship Finals (1961 and 1967) and played Federation Cup (1953-67) and Wightman Cup (1963-67) for most of her career.

Ann Haydon-Jones joined the BBC as a commentator in 1970 and can still be seen during Wimbledon fortnight. She was inducted into the International Tennis Hall of Fame in 1985.

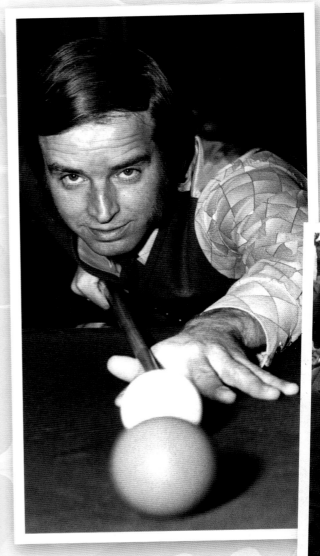

World Snooker Championship reverts to knockout tournament

The climax of the season and the most important event – in terms of world ranking points, prestige and prize money – in snooker's calendar is the World Snooker Championship.

The early years of the Championship were dominated by Joe Davis, who helped to organise the first tournament in 1927. Davis won the inaugural event

and would successfully defend his title until 1946 (there were no competitions between 1941-45 due to the Second World War). His record of 15 titles still stands today.

A disagreement between the governing bodies led to two competitions running side by side from 1952-57. Snooker then hit the doldrums with no tournament being held from 1958 until it was revived on a challenge basis in 1963. This meant that matches took place irregularly – sometimes once a year – and the Championship reverted back to a knockout tournament in 1969, with John Spencer claiming the title.

Above: John Spencer.

REMEMBER THE SIXTIES

Tony Jacklin wins the Open

When Tony Jacklin won the Open Championship in 1969, he became the first British golfer to win on the tournament for 18 years. Not since Max Faulkner triumphed in 1951 had a Briton won on home soil and his US Open victory the following year was the first by a Briton since Ted Ray in 1920. Indeed, such has been the domination of that tournament by other nations that Jacklin's success in the States remains the last by a British golfer since the Second World War.

Jacklin, born in Scunthorpe on 7 July 1944, was the son of a truck driver with a love of the game and it was his father who pushed him to excel at the sport. Tony took up golf at the age of nine. At 13 he won the Lincolnshire Boys Championship and three years later won the Lincolnshire Open by nine shots.

Jacklin turned professional in 1962, becoming assistant to Bill Shankland at Potters Bar, and was Rookie of the Year after finishing 60th in the Order of Merit with earnings of £344.

In 1967, he hit the first televised hole in one in Britain at the 165-yard 16th at Royal St George's, Sandwich before going on to win eight events on the European Tour between 1972-82. He was awarded the OBE in 1970.

A member of the Great Britain and Ireland Ryder Cup team from 1967-77 and of the first European team two years later, Jacklin enjoyed most success as the non-playing captain in four consecutive tournaments between 1983-89. He led his team to their first victory in 28 years over the United States in 1985.

Jacklin announced his retirement from tournament golf in 2004 after finishing tied fourth in the Energis Senior Masters, and is a respected golf course designer.

POLITICS & CURRENT AFFAIRS

Middle East moves

The volatile Middle East saw two new figures in positions of power this year. In February, the Palestine National Congress appointed Yassir Arafat to be the new head of the Palestine Liberation Organisation, while in Israel one-time foreign minister Golda Meir was elected as the next Prime Minister. Arafat had founded resistance movement Fatah in 1963 and had narrowly escaped capture by the Israelis in 1967 when organising cells in Jerusalem.

1960 1961 1962 1963 1964 1965 1966 1967 1968 **1969**

Middle: Tony Jacklin becomes the first British golfer to win the Open Golf Championship for 18 years.
Below: *Yassir Arafat.*

REMEMBER THE SIXTIES

He would henceforth head an 11-man committee organising operations against Israel in the continuing struggle for a Palestinian state. Meir won Israel's highest political office despite the 'handicap' of being a woman and the opposition of defence minister Moshe Dayan – even though he did not stand against her. At 70, the former schoolteacher brought experience to the role, but had suffered ill health that had ended her previous governmental spell.

Arafat died in 2004 without seeing his dream of a Palestinian homeland come true. Meir, who took a hard line toward the Arab world, refusing to stop expansion of settlements in the occupied territories, resigned as PM after the disastrous Yom Kippur War of 1973 and died five years later.

Northern Ireland

After the civil rights marches and loyalist counter-demonstrations in 1968, things seemed initially to be settling down in Northern Ireland. Some effort was made to placate the minority Catholic population, but the peaceful days were not to last, and very soon the province was on its way to a prolonged period of violence and misery.

On New Year's Day 1969, a march across country to Derry was attacked. The violence was to continue for the rest of the year – and for many years afterwards. As 1969 progressed, marches in Northern

Below: British troops patrolling the streets of Belfast during the civil rights riots.